THE WAY
I HEARD IT

THE WAY
I HEARD IT

MIKE ROWE

GALLERY BOOKS

New York   London   Toronto   Sydney   New Delhi

G

Gallery Books
An Imprint of Simon & Schuster, Inc.
1230 Avenue of the Americas
New York, NY 10020

First Gallery Books hardcover edition October 2019

GALLERY BOOKS and colophon are registered trademarks
of Simon & Schuster, Inc.

For information about special discounts for bulk purchases, please contact Simon &
Schuster Special Sales at 1-866-506-1949 or business@simonandschuster.com.

The Simon & Schuster Speakers Bureau can bring authors to your live event. For more
information or to book an event, contact the Simon & Schuster Speakers Bureau at
1-866-248-3049 or visit our website at www.simonspeakers.com.

Interior design by Jaime Putorti
Illustrations by Marcellus Hall

Manufactured in the United States of America

10 9 8 7 6 5 4 3 2 1

Library of Congress Cataloging-in-Publication Data
Names: Rowe, Mike, 1962– author.
Title: The way I heard it / Mike Rowe.
Other titles: Way I heard it (Podcast)
Description: First Gallery Books hardcover edition. | New York : Gallery
  Books, 2019. | Summary: "Emmy-award winning gadfly Mike Rowe presents a
  ridiculously entertaining, seriously fascinating collection of his
  favorite episodes from America's #1 short-form podcast, The Way I Heard
  It, along with a host of memories, ruminations, illustrations, and
  insights. It's a delightful collection of mysteries. A mosaic. A memoir.
  A charming, surprising must-read"—Provided by publisher.
Identifiers: LCCN 2019025244 (print) | LCCN 2019025245 (ebook) | ISBN
  9781982130855 (hardcover) | ISBN 9781982131470 (trade paperback) | ISBN
  9781982130862 (ebook)
Subjects: LCSH: History, Modern—Anecdotes. | United
  States—History—Anecdotes. | Popular culture—United States—Anecdotes.
Classification: LCC D210 .R69 2019 (print) | LCC D210 (ebook) | DDC
  818/.602—dc23
LC record available at https://lccn.loc.gov/2019025244
LC ebook record available at https://lccn.loc.gov/2019025245

ISBN 978-1-9821-3085-5
ISBN 978-1-9821-3086-2 (ebook)

For Mom and Dad . . .
who may have heard it differently

CONTENTS

A promise made is a debt unpaid.

—SAM McGEE

Be wary of all earnestness.

—TRAVIS McGEE

INTRODUCTION

THE WAY I WROTE IT

I drove into the long-term parking lot at BWI twenty-five minutes before my flight was scheduled to depart. This would have been back in 1988. June, I think. I had bags to check and security to clear, but if I hustled, I could still make it. There was just one problem—I couldn't seem to get out of my car. It was the strangest thing. The door wasn't locked, nor was it jammed. In fact, the door was open but I was stuck to my seat, and I remained that way until the man on the radio spoke his magic words. Words that would allow me to grab my bags from the trunk and sprint for the gate. Finally, those words were spoken.

"And now, you know the *rest* of the story."

How many times did I sit in parking lots and driveways long after I'd arrived at my intended destination, waiting for Paul Harvey to utter those words? Too many to count. Thanks to his insanely addictive radio program, *The Rest of the Story,* I missed my flight that day, and ever since, I've wanted to write stories that can't be turned off or put down until the very end. Stories that make people late.

I'll have more to say about Paul Harvey later. For now, I just want to thank him for inspiring *The Way I Heard It,* the podcast whose title is shared by the book you've just begun. Like *The Rest of the Story*, the mysteries in this book tell some true stories you probably don't know, about some famous people you probably do. Your job is to figure out who or what I'm talking about before I get to the end. Inside, you'll find thirty-five mysteries pulled from my podcast. Think of them as tiles in a mosaic. Each of these tiles is followed by a personal recollection. Think of those as the grout that holds the tiles together.

Many of these mysteries were written in the heart of America—in her greasy spoons, hotel rooms, and train stations. Others were composed high above the fruited plain, as I flew hither and yon to host one show or another. Funny thing, though. While writing mysteries up there in the friendly skies, something mysterious happened to me. Time became compressed. Distances started to shrivel. How many times did I begin to write on the tarmac at SFO, only to look up a few minutes later, stunned to be landing at JFK? Too many to count.

Picture me at 37,000 feet . . .

My laptop is open, the light is on above me, and everyone around me is sleeping. That's what I pictured for the photo on the cover of this book: me in a middle seat, writing the words you're reading today. I went with a corner diner instead because the food's better, but you get the idea—half of this book was written on the road. The other half—the grout—was mixed right here, at my kitchen table.

Perhaps you can picture that, too?

A fire snaps and crackles in the background, the fog blows in from under the Golden Gate, and my faithful dog, Freddy, gnaws on my slippers as I wrestle with the question gnawing at me—why, exactly, did I write about the people I wrote about? I mean, *something* must have drawn me toward the subjects I'd picked, right? The more I considered what that something was, the more I discovered some surprising connections—personal connections that I hadn't noticed from 37,000 feet or at the lunch counter at Mel's. Invariably, these connections began to rhyme, and soon the mosaic began to change. The grout and the tiles became equally important.

How many times did I look up from my laptop, only to see that the fire had gone out, the dog was asleep, the fog was gone, and the moon was right where the sun had been shining just moments ago? Too many to count.

You've already met Freddy, and you'll run across him again in the pages to come. He's a good boy. You'll meet my parents, my girl-friend, and my high-school mentor. There will be ghosts and pigs, farmers and fishermen, movie stars, presidents, Nazis, and bloody do-gooders, along with the fictitious knight-errant upon whom my entire worldview was once based. Along the way, you'll hear stories about *Dirty Jobs* and a long list of less notable shows that still haunt me on YouTube. Shows I've tried to forget, but cannot. In all cases, each story is told *the way I heard it*. If you've heard it differently, I'm okay with that, and I hope you are, too.

By the way, I'm trying to picture you, too. Is that creepy? I hope not.

I see you checking in to some quaint bed-and-breakfast—in Oregon, maybe, or Texas, or even in England or France. You've arrived late, worn out from your journey. You've built a fire and slipped into bed. This book, dog-eared and stained, just happens to be the one lying on your bedside table. You pick it up. You start to read. And when you look up, the fog is gone, the fire is out, and there's the sun, right where the moon was just moments ago. You wonder where the night went.

On Monday morning, at the water cooler, you might share one of these stories with a friend. They'll probably raise an eyebrow and say, "Wow! Is that really the way it happened?" If I were you, I'd say: "You better believe it. At least . . . that's the way *I* heard it."

THIS ISN'T FUNNY

Corporal Kaminsky was precariously perched atop a makeshift utility pole, forty feet above the frozen ground. In the dim light of a crescent moon, he squinted to complete his task and tried not to lose his battle with gravity.

As a member of the 1104th Engineer Combat Group, Kaminsky was used to such work. What he was *not* used to was doing it so close to the enemy. You see, the particular pole to which this particular corporal clung was planted in Belgium. Specifically, in the Ardennes Forest. Just through the trees, a big chunk of the German Army was preparing to launch an enormous offensive that would be remembered, forever, as the Battle of the Bulge.

They were so close Kaminsky could smell them: an odorous stew of gasoline, bratwurst, and boiled cabbage filled his nostrils. He could *hear* them, too. They'd been playing propaganda recordings all night long: an unholy mix of the German national anthem, the latest ravings of the mad Führer, and the sweet voice of Axis Sally, urging our boys to lay down their guns and surrender.

As he twisted the last wire around the last screw that would carry the current to a slightly different broadcast, he heard a harsh whisper from the sentry below him. "This isn't funny, Kaminsky!" That made the young corporal smile. If there was one thing he'd learned growing up on the mean streets of Brooklyn, it was this: whenever anyone said "that's not funny," it was almost certain to be hilarious.

Kaminsky shimmied down the pole, took one last glance up at the enormous loudspeaker he'd just installed, and chuckled. The sentry shook his head as Kaminsky scurried back to battalion command.

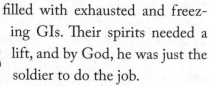

Along the way he stepped around numerous foxholes filled with exhausted and freezing GIs. Their spirits needed a lift, and by God, he was just the soldier to do the job.

Kaminsky searched through a small box of vinyl 78s, looking for the perfect selection for an occasion such as this. His eyes settled on a classic, and he chuckled again.

A switch was flipped, a dial was cranked, and the wall of sound that erupted from Kaminsky's loudspeaker echoed through the frozen forest. In an instant, the racist rantings of Adolf Hitler were drowned out by the unmistakable refrain known to millions:

Toot, Toot, Tootsie, goodbye!
Toot, Toot, Tootsie, don't cry!

For several glorious and confusing minutes, the only thing the soldiers on either side could hear were the dulcet tones of the one and only . . . Al Jolson. Who, like Corporal Kaminsky, just happened to be . . . very, very Jewish.

Kaminsky watched the war-torn boys poke their heads out of their foxholes like curious prairie dogs. The absurdity of the situation took a few moments to process, but soon the irony washed over the troops and laughter set in. Nazis, in the middle of a battlefield, driven by their insane hatred of Jews, were being serenaded by one. Now, *that* was funny!

I guess if you can make people laugh on the battlefields of Europe, you can make people laugh anywhere. And that had always been Corporal Kaminsky's goal. After the war he found work as a writer and comedian. For the next twenty years, he made a name for himself in Tinseltown. Finally, he got a chance to do what he had been born to do: direct.

His first effort nearly gave the studio a heart attack. It was a screenplay he had written himself, but the suits were not amused. "That is *not* funny," they said. But of course Kaminsky knew exactly what that meant: he had a winner! He stood by his guns. He dug in his heels. Before long, Americans were tapping their toes to catchy numbers like "Springtime for Hitler" and punchy lyrics like "Don't be stupid, be a smarty, come and join the Nazi Party!"

Maybe it *was* in bad taste. Maybe it *was* too soon. But all those put off by Kaminsky's directorial debut were soon afforded more opportunities to be offended—on the big screen, the small screen, and of course the Great White Way. Because even though Melvin Kaminsky changed his name, he never changed his tune. In Belgium, he'd confronted hatred with a song and dance. In New York and Hollywood, he doubled down. Today, *The Producers* is considered to be one of the greatest comedies of all time. And the funniest corporal of all time? That's easy. That would be the always improper, always tasteless, never appropriate . . . Mel Brooks.

Anyway, that's the way I heard it.

I never played "Toot, Toot, Tootsie" in a forest filled with Nazis. But with the help of three high school pals, I did sing it, in four-part harmony, for a variety of captive audiences in Baltimore, Maryland. Nursing homes were our favorite venue, followed in no particular order by hospitals, bathrooms, VFW halls, prisons, elevators, stairwells, and crowded restaurants.

Why, you ask? Why were four teenage boys terrorizing an unsuspecting public in 1979 with songs written decades before we were born?

Two words: Fred King.

At Overlea High School in Baltimore, our larger-than-life music teacher, Mr. King, had introduced us to the mysterious pleasures of barbershop harmony. Mr. King himself had been a legendary baritone in a quartet called the Oriole Four; he was known, in the trade, as the "King of the Barbershoppers." Under his tutelage, we amassed an impressive repertoire of chestnuts like "Margie," "Lida Rose," "The Sunshine of Your Smile," and "Sweet Adeline"— unapologetically sentimental tunes that might have made other teenagers cringe. But we loved those songs, and we quickly formed our own group.

We called ourselves "Semi-Fourmal" because we wore tuxedos and tennis shoes. We misspelled "formal" intentionally, because there were four of us and we were terribly clever. Chuck sang lead. I sang bass. Bobby and Mike sang baritone and tenor, respectively. Soon we became the youngest members of the oldest men's chorus in the country—the world champion Chorus of the Chesapeake, which Fred King also directed.

Every Tuesday night, a hundred men from all walks of life gathered in the old gymnasium at Johns Hopkins Hospital. Doctors, carpenters, lawyers, plumbers, accountants, dentists, teachers, Democrats, Republicans, Protestants, Catholics, Jews—a cross section of men whose deep love of four-part harmony was rivaled only by their deep love of God, country, and beer. I'll never forget the first time I heard them sing. The Nazis might have been stunned by the sound of "Toot, Toot, Tootsie" blaring through the forest on that cold winter night, but the sound of a hundred men singing that same song in perfect harmony would have left them gobsmacked. It was a sound unlike anything I'd ever heard. A sound that filled the air with overtones that buzzed and crackled. A sound so rich and full and unmistakably masculine, it made the hairs on your arms stand on end.

Ultimately, it was the sound that pulled me into show business.

After rehearsal, we'd follow the men over to a Highlandtown bar called Johnny Jones for another kind of singing. They called it "woodshedding," because a woodshed—far away from the ears of innocent civilians—was the only sensible place to do it. Improvisational harmonizing isn't always pretty. But it's fun to do and a fine way to learn the old songs. Johnny's had a space crammed with square tables—just the right amount of room for four men to harmonize at point-blank range. Johnny himself would pour beer without thinking to ask for my age, pitch pipes would blow in various keys, and various quartets would sing various songs simultaneously. There were songs about mothers and flying machines and pals who would never let you down. There were patriotic songs, as well as songs about sweethearts, punctuated with bottomless pitchers of draft beer and Maryland crab cakes. It was a soundtrack from another time, and in between the cacophony, the men lit their pipes and told their stories. Oftentimes, war stories.

Kids today think they know everything. Back in 1979, we were no different. But after a few visits to Johnny's, I began to think differently about the cost of freedom. That'll happen, I guess, when you harmonize with men who actually fought in that terrible battle that began in Belgium on December 16, 1944. Along with the dead and the wounded, 23,000 US soldiers went missing in the Battle of the Bulge. That fact I learned from an old tenor named Gus, who for a time had been among the missing. He was just seventeen in 1944, the same age as me when we met in 1979—and he'd actually been there, in the Ardennes, doing things in that dark forest on my behalf that I would never be asked to do. Brave men like Gus had learned the hard way what I came to know simply by standing beside them and singing: You're only as good as the man next to you.

But then, Mel Brooks would tell you that courage is a funny thing. You never know where you'll find it. Or whether *you'll* have it, on the day you need it the most.

A HERO UNDER
THE INFLUENCE

Like everyone else at ground zero, Charlie was in the wrong place at the wrong time. He'd spent all day in the kitchen, overseeing a crew of thirteen junior bakers, churning out breads and cakes and pies and pastries for a crowd that never seemed to dwindle. Charlie had always hoped to make a name for himself in a famous kitchen. He'd headed off to a faraway, famous city armed with dreams of success. Now those dreams were coming true. As the chief baker in one of the world's premier restaurants, Charlie was practicing the trade he loved and devoted to pleasing his customers.

To be clear, Charlie was drunk on the day in question. His blood alcohol content a few hours after impact would have confirmed an almost inconceivable rate of consumption. But that's the point—Charlie's drinking did *not* precede the impact—it followed it. And really, who can blame him? When the walls and floor shuddered around him, Charlie knew something had slammed into the towering structure—something big. And when he saw the extent of the damage, he didn't panic. He merely retired to the bar of his now empty restaurant to enjoy what he knew would be the last drink of

his life. But what exactly does one
drink as one ponders one's own
mortality and considers one's
final actions on Earth?

For Charlie, the options
were endless. From the finest
champagnes to the very best
Italian wines, they were all
there for the sampling—
and Charlie sampled them
all. There were Beaujolais
and sherry, Drambuie
and absinthe, cognac and
Armagnac, endless rows
of schnapps, and beers
from around the world. Mostly, though, there was some old Irish
whiskey. Ah, yes. That was just what the doctor ordered. The perfect
elixir to prepare Charlie for the job at hand—the job he believed he
was duty bound to execute.

Charlie pounded half the bottle and poured the rest into a large
flask. Then he filled a sack with breads and pastries and made his
way slowly up to the top floor. Elevators were not an option, so he
took the stairs, encountering dozens of panicked customers along
the way—people who just a few hours before had been sitting in
his restaurant, eating his cakes and pies, luxuriating in five-star
elegance.

"Follow me," he said. "I know the way out."

Up top, it was pandemonium. Charlie did everything he could
to calm his customers. First he handed out his pastries. Then he
offered shots of courage from his bottomless flask. When it became
obvious that the first responders weren't responding, he did what
he knew had to be done—he began to push his customers over the
edge. Understandably, many resisted, but Charlie knew there was

no other way out. He grabbed them, one after the next, and heaved them over the side. But when the opportunity came for him to follow suit, he said, "No." He grabbed another customer from the panicked crowd and insisted she go in his place.

If you've seen the movie, you might recall the dramatic finale—two lovers, standing on the pinnacle of that doomed and crumbling edifice, waiting for the inevitable collapse. Well, those lovers weren't really there—but the chief baker was. Charles Joughin, filled with adrenaline and booze, had taken it upon himself to fill multiple lifeboats with dozens of terrified women and children, all of whom were loath to leave their husbands and fathers behind. Then—defying the laws of gravity and the basic rules of intoxication—the inebriated baker crawled over the side and scampered all the way up to what must have felt like the top of the world. There, flask in hand, he rode the ruined remains all the way down, waiting until the last possible second before stepping from his perch into the 28-degree water.

He should have died, just like everyone else who didn't make it into a lifeboat. But he didn't. He splashed around the North Atlantic for three hours, until the *Carpathia* finally arrived and plucked him out of the black, icy sea with little more than two swollen feet and a lingering buzz. It was the booze, they said, that had kept him alive, thinning his blood to the point where hypothermia was kept at bay.

If James Cameron had allowed Leonardo DiCaprio a few slugs of whiskey, his character, too, might have survived that terrible night and grown old with Kate Winslet. But of course there was no happy ending for Jack and Rose, or for the 1,500 real people who perished on their way to New York City. Thanks to an open and unguarded bar, Charles Joughin was not among them. He was busy putting his customers first and preparing to step into history as the inebriated baker who just happened to be the very last person to abandon . . . the *Titanic*.

Of all the dreadful details to fixate upon, I think about the conditions at the time of the sinking. No wind. No waves. Dead calm. According to every account, the Atlantic was flat when the great ship went down. Flat and black like a duck pond—a dark mirror with no reflection. How terrifying must it have been to be slowly pulled beneath that tranquil surface? How terrible for the captain, who knew he'd been driving the ship too fast?

In 2004, seven years after Leonardo DiCaprio sank to the bottom of James Cameron's sea, the Discovery Channel invited me to host a documentary called *Deadliest Catch*.

"It's not really 'on brand,'" they told me. "It'll never go to series. But at least you won't be crawling through sewers!"

I get suspicious when network executives tell me what their "brand" is. Seems to me your "brand" should be whatever your viewers are willing to watch. But I was happy for the work and eager to see Alaska.

"Why are you calling it *Deadliest Catch*?"

"Crab fishing is dangerous," the executives said. "Plus it's a snappy title."

I chuckled. I had grown up fishing for blue crab on the Chesapeake Bay. Tying raw chicken necks to long strands of twine, tossing the bait off the end of the dock, reeling in the crabs as they clung to the poultry, and watching my brother scoop them up into his net. Yeah, I knew all about crab fishing. How dangerous could it be?

I arrived in Dutch Harbor a few days after Thanksgiving. The flight had taken me from San Francisco to Seattle, which was pleasant; Seattle to Anchorage, which was also pleasant; and then over the vast Bering Sea to Dutch Harbor, which was not pleasant. Not pleasant at all.

Technically, I guess it was turbulence, but not the kind I'd experienced in the lower forty-eight. It was a kind of turbulence unique to islands with big hills that flank narrow runways buffeted by constant crosswinds. It snapped the overhead compartments open. It sent a beverage cart careening down the aisle. It was the kind of turbulence that would make a plane full of hardened fishermen blubber and curse and pray, all at the same time.

A hundred feet before touching down, our pilot aborted the landing and flew to Cold Bay, where he put the plane down on a runway that had been built for the space shuttle. We spent twenty-four hours there waiting for the weather to clear, enjoying a variety of stale treats from vending machines in the empty airport.

When I finally did arrive in Dutch, I headed straight to the docks, where the film crew was waiting to board a crab boat. Was it the *Fierce Allegiance*? The *Maverick*? The *Bountiful*? I don't remember. What I do remember is that the rain was blowing sideways and turning to sleet as I climbed aboard. Remember, it was 2004, and all I knew then was that I was hosting a documentary about crab fishing. I didn't know what the show would become. *No one* knew. But the director wanted footage of me baiting the massive 800-pound pots and chatting with the crew, giving the viewer a sense of how crab boats worked on the open ocean. It was an odd role to assume: part host, part greenhorn, part reporter—a strange combination that left the deckhands confused as to what my actual purpose on their boat was. It was a confusion I shared.

Twenty miles out of Dutch, things got sporty. Green water rolled over the bow as we plunged under wave after wave in twelve-foot seas. The wind picked up, I threw up—the waves got bigger and bigger—but the work never stopped. In the wheelhouse, the captain kept a lit cigarette in each hand even as one dangled from his mouth. He looked like a human chimney. On deck, the massive, 800-pound pots slid back and forth as the swells built around us. It was an impossible situation to shoot, and our attempts to do so annoyed the captain and crew. I recalled the terrific line at the start of *Ulysses*: "The sea, the snotgreen sea, the scrotumtightening sea."

I survived, and by Christmas I had actually gotten used to the snotgreen sea. By New Year's Day, my scrotum had returned to its normal state. It might have remained that way but for the events of January 15, when the weather did something truly terrifying. The wind stopped howling, the waves stopped rolling, and the temperature rose to a balmy 30 degrees. For the first time all month the Bering Sea . . . settled down.

The boat that sank that day was called the *Big Valley*. She slipped beneath the surface while I was sleeping back at the hotel. Conditions were not to blame. In fact, when the ship left port, the Bering Sea was flat and black, like a duck pond—a dark mirror with no reflection. Maybe that's why the captain went out with too many pots. Far too many. But the Bering Sea is an unpredictable place, and when the wind picked up, the *Big Valley* became unstable. A death trap. Six men perished as a result, seventy miles off St. Paul Island.

How terrifying must it have been, to be slowly pulled beneath the surface? How terrible for the captain, who knew his boat had been carrying too much weight?

I can still picture the faces of men I met a week later at the memorial—hardened fishermen who blubbered and cursed and prayed, all at the same time. *Deadliest Catch* had lived up to its name, I suppose, but it had done so in ways that we'd never imagined or wanted. Ways that haunt me to this day.

ON THE IMPORTANCE OF BETTER DRIVING

Back in May 1932, a sixty-one-year-old handyman named John Thompson was tinkering in his garage when he had himself a Eureka moment—a self-centered idea that would virtually eliminate bad driving. In those days, bad driving was commonplace, and US automakers weren't sure what to do about it. But Thompson believed the problem had less to do with bad drivers and more to do with the obstacles they encountered—specifically, recessed gullies, intricate curves, and flat horizontal planes. His idea would promote better driving by eliminating those obstacles.

Six months later, he had a gleaming prototype in his garage, ready for action. Six months after that, Patent no. 1,080,080 arrived in the US mail, making him the sole owner of the device that would virtually eliminate bad driving. All he needed now was someone to mass-produce it.

John traveled all over the United States looking for a manufacturing partner. He visited dozens of factories and presented his prototype to countless engineers. The reaction was always the same: "Great idea, Mr. Thompson. But no, thanks."

After two years of "no," John grew discouraged. He'd never tried to sell anything before, and the rejections were demoralizing. He made his last pitch in a conference room full of engineers at a manu- facturing facility in Oregon.

"Good morning, Mr. Thompson. We're intrigued by your design. The cruciform, the conical helix, and the self-centering aspect are most innovative. But please explain to us how such a thing can be mass-produced."

"Well," John said with a nervous laugh, "I was hoping that's what you fellas could tell me."

The engineers said nothing, so John plunged in. He talked about the fundamental problem—the frequency with which drivers wound up getting stuck—and the inevitable damage that followed when they continued to accelerate. Then he explained how his device would solve the problem by ejecting the driver before the moment of impact. When he was done, the engineers all agreed: his idea was brilliant but simply too hard to mass-produce. In other words, "No, thanks."

Later that evening, belly to the bar, John was staring at the dia- grams on the wrinkled pages of his worthless patent when a man with white teeth and perfect hair struck up a conversation.

"Don't take it so hard, friend. A 'no' is just a 'yes' to a different question!"

"Spare me the platitudes," John said. "I know what a 'no' means. I hear it every day."

The man's name was Henry. He grinned, pulled up a stool, and ordered a fresh round of drinks. "What exactly are you trying to sell?"

John handed Henry his patent. Henry didn't understand all the details, but he knew the importance of better driving. He offered to buy one more round. Then he offered to buy John's idea for a handful of cash. John agreed, and after that, things happened fast.

Henry returned to the company that had just rejected John's idea and asked to see the president, a man named Eugene Clark. "Oh, no," said the secretary. "Not without an appointment."

But Clark's secretary didn't understand that a "no" was just a "yes" to another question. Henry smiled his charming smile and showed her the patent he'd bought. "This idea is going to eliminate driver error," he said. "I can show it to a competitor, but wouldn't you rather show it to the boss yourself?"

The secretary looked at the patent. Like Henry, she didn't understand all the details but knew the importance of better driving. She showed the patent to her boss, and soon Henry was sitting across from the president of the company, stretching the truth a bit and posing additional questions that could be answered only in the affirmative.

"Mr. Clark, I just heard from General Motors. They want millions of these things. Your engineers say it can't be done. Should I ask someone else to give it a try, or do you want to give it another shot?"

Clark picked up the phone and summoned his engineers back to the conference room. Once again the engineers examined the prototype and said "No." They blamed the practical limits of a cold steel forge and the many challenges of scaling a product of this size. But the engineers didn't realize that a "no" was just a "yes" to another question. When Clark asked if they wanted to keep their jobs, they went back to the drawing board and *did* come up with a way to mass-produce Henry's prototype. At which point Henry flew to Detroit to persuade General Motors to place a massive order for a million devices that did not yet exist.

You can guess what happened next. Henry got a meeting with the president of General Motors and persuaded him to test the prototype. Driver performance improved dramatically, and General Motors offered to buy Henry's idea. But this time, it was Henry who said "No." Because Henry had no intention of selling his driving system to just anybody. He wanted to license it—to *everybody*.

Ultimately, General Motors ordered millions. Then Chrysler. Then Ford. Then the Department of Defense. Henry's patented technology wound up inside every new car on America's highways. Henry's bank account? That wound up packed with $65 million in today's dollars. And as for John Thompson?

He got screwed.

There's really no other way to put it. The aging handyman had been right all along. He knew the problem with bad driving had less to do with the drivers themselves and more to do with the obstacles they encountered. He was the one who replaced those troublesome gullies with a unique, tapered cruciform. He was the one who looked at those horizontal planes and saw what an ingenious conical helix could do. His patented Self-Centering Drive System solved the chronic problem of over-torquing—by automatically ejecting drivers before they could cause any serious damage. Not human drivers. *Mechanical* drivers. *That* was the breakthrough that dramatically increased the speed and productivity of American assembly lines. But the breakthrough was not named for the man who invented or designed it. It was named for the man who bought it and sold it— over and over and over again.

A salesman who knew that a "no" was just a "yes" to a different question.

A guy named Henry, whose last name is still synonymous with the screw that made him rich and the screwdriver that made him famous . . . Phillips.

Over the years, I've had the good fortune to speak on behalf of some pretty remarkable companies: Ford, Caterpillar, Discovery, Hewlett-Packard, and Motorola, to brag ever so humbly about a few. But long before I became "the Ford guy," I was selling water purifiers door to door and magazine subscriptions over the phone and hosting infomercials. I was also hawking a variety of dubious products between the hours of 3:00 and 6:00 a.m., on the QVC cable shopping channel.

Back in 1990, QVC was having difficulty recruiting show

hosts. Experienced salespeople weren't comfortable on TV. Experienced TV people weren't comfortable selling things. So QVC stopped hiring experienced people—and started hiring people who could talk about a pencil for eight minutes. That was the audition, and for reasons that would probably take a psychiatrist to unpack, I was able to discuss the features and benefits of a Dixon Ticonderoga no. 2 ad nauseam. I was hired and placed on the graveyard shift for the three-month nocturnal crucible called "the probationary period."

In hindsight, it was a fantastic way to learn: three hours of live TV without a script. With no prompter, no delay, and almost no supervision. Just a producer named Marty, a former host who slumbered at his desk while I worked. For me, it was a true baptism by fire, partly because I'd never been on TV before and partly because there was no real training program. Aspiring hosts were left to figure out for themselves how best to discuss the bewildering array of products they were charged with presenting.

On my first shift, I walked onto the set at precisely 3:00 a.m. Four robotic cameras faced me, controlled by a crew of operators hidden behind a pane of smoked glass twenty yards away. I sat behind a desk on a pie-shaped stage that rotated every hour to reveal a new setting from which to hawk new categories of pabulum. That particular hour was called *Ideas for Your Home*. What type of home? Hard to say, given the products I'd been asked to sell. Every five minutes or so a stagehand would bring me some gadget I'd never encountered before: the Amcor negative ion generator; a hand-painted Hummel figurine; the first cordless phone I'd ever seen; the first karaoke machine. The supply of products was endless, and the products themselves were profoundly unfamiliar.

I began with something called a Katsak, a paper grocery bag lined with Mylar, guaranteed to make a "crinkling" sound cats supposedly find "irresistible." Yes, it's a real thing. It's out there, online.

You can actually watch me trying to sell this thing on YouTube—talking about the Katsak for ten whole minutes.

No one bought any.

Then they brought me a lava lamp, which I attempted to open on the air to see if there was lava inside. There wasn't. No one bought any of those, either.

Then they brought me something called the Healthteam Infrared Pain Reliever. It looked like a miniature flashlight with a cord attached. It cost $29.99 and promised to "relieve arthritic pain with healing infrared light when applied directly to the troubled area."

With eight minutes left on the clock and not one cogent thing in my head, I looked into the camera and said, "Folks, I'm gonna be honest with you: I have no idea what this thing is or how it works. Frankly, I'm skeptical about the healing power of infrared light. But if you have one of these objects, call the 800 number on the screen. Ask for Marty. He'll put you on the air. Maybe you can tell me if it actually works."

Ten seconds later, something extraordinary happened. Someone called in. A nice lady named Carol explained exactly what the product did and told me she was very satisfied with hers. She also told me I had pretty eyes. After that, things got weird but more fun. With each new product, more viewers called in to explain what the gadget was and how it worked. These were not "testimonials"; these were tutorials. The viewers had taken pity on me and begun to do my job for me. Sales picked up. Marty woke up. Like I said, things got fun.

Years later, while narrating a nature documentary, I learned that young wolves, when confronted with bigger, stronger wolves, will sometimes roll onto their backs and expose their bellies. According to the narrator, the submissive posture they adopt is a way for weaker wolves to show they're not a threat. According to my veterinarian,

this is the same reason my dog pees on me when I come home: he "respects my authority." I'm not sure I buy that. In fact, I'm pretty sure Freddy is just incontinent. But I do believe there's more than one way to sell something. For me, the secret was to admit my vulnerability on camera and quit pretending that I knew more than I did. To adopt my own submissive posture.

NO POLITE WAY TO PUT IT

George was horny. Sorry to be indelicate, but there's really no polite way to put it. He hadn't seen Elizabeth in weeks, and he missed his wife with the white-hot intensity of a thousand suns.

"Excuse me, sir, but a letter has arrived."

George leapt from his chair and ran to the doorway. "Hand it over, my good man, with all due speed."

The courier complied. George locked the door behind him. With trembling hands, he opened the envelope. The sight of her hand-writing quickened his pulse. The smell of her perfume wafted from the page, leaving him light-headed and breathless.

"Oh, my gallant champion," it began. "How I miss you. If only we could be together, for just a few hours. If only I could sit 'Tomboy' for a quick ride with you behind me."

George swallowed hard, gripping the page with his free hand. By God, his wife really could turn a phrase! He tried to slow things down, but when he got to the part that read, "I know of a soft place upon some-body's carpet, that yearns for a gentle touch," well, that was simply too much. George had to . . . collect himself, then start again from the top.

The second time was better. It always was. George read more slowly now, with as much patience as he could muster. He savored every syllable, pausing between paragraphs to fully embrace the images his wife had so cleverly evoked. When he finished, he wiped the perspiration from his brow and tried to return the favor.

"Good morning, my Rosebud," he wrote. "'Little John' has been making constant and earnest inquiries for his bunkey for a very long time, and this morning, he seems more persistent than ever. I, too, yearn to be in the saddle behind you, holding on for dear life! And yes—I know just *where* I'd kiss a certain someone, if I was with her tonight."

Two weeks later, his letter arrived in Monroe, Michigan. A butler delivered it to the boudoir. There Elizabeth devoured his words in much the same way he had devoured hers. Hungrily. Greedily. Then—after multiple readings—she reached for her pen and paper and got busy crafting another flurry of phrases carefully concocted to help her husband . . . release the tension . . . during their long periods of separation. In other words, George and Elizabeth were sexting, Victorian style.

Sorry to be indelicate, but there's really no polite way to put it. Their letters were the nineteenth-century equivalent of naked selfies, packed with double entendres that would have made Anthony Weiner blush. There were references to "long, extended gallops" and "riding under the crupper." In one letter, Elizabeth alluded to the possibility of "breaking in a new filly" for their "mutual pleasure" and discussed the pros and cons of being "ridden hard and put away wet."

True, George was a famous equestrian—but no one would have mistaken the topic in question. And of course, no one did. Because George wasn't just a horny husband, he was a careless husband. At a time when a man's reputation and a woman's virtue were still fragile, important things, George failed to protect both.

One day, Elizabeth's letters were stolen. They appeared in the pages of the *Richmond Gazette*. Before long, the entire country was reading all about "Little John," the pleasures of riding "Tomboy," and that "soft place upon someone's carpet," in need of a gentle touch.

One can only imagine how Elizabeth must have felt, seeing her words in print. Yet she survived the scandal. Over time, people forgot all about it. Likewise, they lost sight of her husband's other shortcomings. They forgot about his impetuous nature. They forgot about his need to always be the center of attention. They forgot about those things because, once again, Elizabeth put pen to paper, extolling the virtues of her husband in a series of wildly popular books about his life on the frontier and his exploits on the battlefield. By the time she died, at the advanced age of ninety, she had single-handedly transformed George's reputation—not from that of a careless husband who'd famously embarrassed his wife, but from that of a famous commander who'd carelessly killed his own men.

In the movie, George dies with his boots on, fighting heroically right up to the bitter end. In real life, no one knows. His body was found three days after the smoke cleared—naked, blackened, bloated, and covered with flies. Some said a finger had been cut off and taken as a souvenir. Others said his eardrums had been pierced with a sewing needle: punishment for his "failure to listen." Some said that he appeared to be smiling (as the dead often do), while one claimed an arrow had been (forgive me) forced into his rectum, pushed through his intestines and into his "Little John," leaving his corpse in a state of perpetual readiness, even as it putrefied under the blue Montana sky.

Sorry to be indelicate, but there's really no polite way to put it. Some of George's men were skinned alive. Others were dismembered and rearranged on the ground. President Ulysses S. Grant called the entire debacle "an abominable, totally unnecessary slaughter caused by the stupidity and rashness of a vain, corkheaded fool." But despite all that, the soldier who marched his men into the valley of death is remembered today as an enduring hero of the American West— thanks to a devoted wife who never stopped grieving, never stopped writing, and never stopped believing her horny husband was some kind of hero, in spite of his unforgivable arrogance on the banks of a river called Little Bighorn.

Not exactly a happy ending for the impatient Boy General but a far better legacy than he deserved, thanks to the blushing bride he left behind—a best-selling author named . . . Elizabeth Custer.

———————

I thought about Custer not long ago, at a watering hole called Grumpy's, after narrating another few episodes of *How the Universe Works* for my friends at the Science Channel. I've learned many interesting things narrating that series, starting with the undeniable fact that I'm going to die in the grip of a cold, indifferent cosmos. The only uncertainty seems to revolve around the exact method of my inevitable demise. What will it be? A supermassive black hole? The collision of two neutron stars? A supernova? A comet? An asteroid? Gamma rays?

Is it any wonder that after a long day of this stuff, I typically end up at Grumpy's?

On that particular day, I had introduced my audience to the

existence of "strangelets"—killer particles that "zombify" matter, whatever that means. I wasn't blasé about it. As a narrator of some experience, I infused the copy with an appropriate level of certainty as I reminded my terrified viewers that no one is going to get out of this thing alive.

Then again, was I right to sound so certain?

From time to time (more times than you might imagine), the Science Channel calls me back to the booth to rerecord something I've read in an earlier episode—not because I've screwed up (which *never* happens), but because new information has been discovered that contradicts claims made in previous scripts. Once, I was asked to rerecord a passage that made reference to the total number of galaxies in the cosmos. I had originally announced, in a crisp, well-modulated baritone, that there were "approximately one hundred billion galaxies in the known universe."

I remember thinking "Damn, that's a lot of galaxies"—and again, being a narrator of some experience, I infused the copy with what I felt to be an appropriate level of certainty and gravitas.

Well, a week later, I was called back to the booth. Turns out, a new method of measuring the cosmos had led astronomers to revise the number of galaxies in the known universe from one hundred billion to two *trillion*. In a single week, we'd found another *two thousand billion* galaxies. But as I reread the new copy, I was struck by the undeniable fact that I sound no less certain when I'm right than I do when I'm wrong.

I don't want to overstate things, but the facts are clear: millions, or billions—for all I know, trillions—of people tune in every week to hear me explain the workings of our universe. It's hard to say, in these uncertain times. But there are no soldiers among my undoubtedly vast audience, waiting to follow me into battle. Custer had six hundred men behind him—the whole 7th Regiment—hanging on his every word. I can't help but wonder: How certain did Custer sound, under a big, blue Montana sky, when he led his men into that valley of death?

Alas, there was no recording booth for Custer to be called back to. There were no do-overs for him and his men. Just the knife, the arrow, and the tomahawk.

Of that, at least, I am certain.

A PATIENT MAN

John was a patient man. His attraction to Peggy had been instantaneous and profound; their courtship, a whirlwind of barely suppressed passion. And now, as John stood at the altar, watching the object of his affection walk slowly toward him, his thoughts were those of a man whose patience was finally about to pay off.

As Peggy drew ever closer and the organ heralded the coming of the bride, John recalled the day he'd proposed. At first Peggy had demurred. She'd said she'd "think about it tomorrow." But John was persistent as well as patient, and eventually she said "Yes." How happy he had been. How relieved. He knew that the most eligible debutante in Atlanta had accepted proposals from five other men—all with more to offer than he could ever hope to match. He knew that she had broken off all those engagements. But now here they were: Peggy in her wedding gown and John in his tuxedo, standing just a few feet apart.

The ceremony was a blur. Scriptures were quoted, songs were sung, the minister spoke sacred words, and all of Atlanta's society bore witness. Then the tricky part came. Before he got to the vows, the minister regarded the congregation and invited anyone present who might object to the union to speak now or forever hold their peace.

John glanced out at the faces of those assembled in the crowded church and held his breath. He knew that several of Peggy's previous suitors were in attendance. Would they object? What would he do if they did?

The moment passed. John exhaled, slowly. And when the minister asked the groom if he would "love, honor, and cherish Peggy from this day forward," John stared into the face of his true love and said the only thing that he could say: nothing. Because the preacher was

not talking to John. The preacher was talking to John's best friend, a man named Berrien Upshaw—Red to his friends. Today, Red was the man that Peggy was marrying.

John had plenty of objections, but disinclined as he was to "forever hold his peace," he had no intention of "speaking now." He proceeded with his plan instead. He smiled. He handed Red the wedding band and applauded as his best friend married the love of his life.

The following days, weeks, and months were difficult for John. He knew his true love was in the arms of another man. But John couldn't really blame Peggy. Red was a charmer. He looked like a film star. He'd made a fortune as a Prohibition-era bootlegger, and he possessed a mercurial quality that made him irresistible to the fairer sex. John Marsh, on the other hand, was a mild-mannered public relations man who dabbled in journalism. As Peggy had told John when she broke their engagement, along with his heart, "Life is under no obligation to give us what we expect."

Indeed.

But with respect to expectations, John knew something that Red and Peggy did not. He knew . . . them. He knew them better than they knew themselves or each other.

John knew that Red expected a compliant and cooperative wife. He knew that Peggy expected a tolerant and devoted husband. In time, John believed, their expectations would go unmet—and when they did, he knew that Red Upshaw would no longer give a damn about his sacred vows. He'd be more likely to give his blushing bride a whack. And Peggy would never tolerate that.

Two months went by before Red ran out of patience with the fiery woman who couldn't help but speak her mind. When she showed him a bit too much sass, he showed her the back of his hand—and that was that. Peggy moved out, and John was waiting to pick up the pieces. Before long, he proposed again. Peggy told him she'd think about it . . . tomorrow.

John smiled and said he'd heard that one yesterday. Peggy smiled back, and this time she said "Yes" straightaway. They lived happily ever after.

Sadly, "ever after" would last only twenty-four years. Peggy was killed by a drunk driver when she was just forty-eight. But during her time with John, she didn't just find true love; she found her true voice. With John's encouragement, Peggy started to write. She wrote about love and passion, pride and prejudice, war and death, hope, and all the things in between. Some say she wrote the story of her own life.

Peggy never confirmed that. But then again, the most famous character she created was a strong-willed southern belle: a beautiful socialite named Pansy, whom every man wanted to wed. Peggy swore up and down that Pansy had nothing to do with her. But she did choose for Pansy's husband a dashing, mercurial bootlegger—who, she swore, had nothing to do with Red. As for the character Pansy desired but could never possess—a man married to her best friend? Nope, that guy wasn't inspired by John Marsh. Not at all.

Whatever the truth was, the publishers loved Peggy's manuscript. They did have one change to make when it came to the 1,037-page novel, which went on to win the Pulitzer Prize and sold 30 million copies in the process. They thought the name "Pansy" was too weak for the fiery character Peggy had pulled from thin air—and John convinced Peggy that the publishers were right.

In real life, that's exactly how it happened. A dashing bootlegger named Red Upshaw frankly didn't give a damn—while an average Joe named John Marsh knew with certainty that tomorrow would be another day. As for Margaret Mitchell—she'd written herself as a Pansy, though her publisher knew she was really a Scarlett. And as for everything else, well, that's . . . *Gone with the Wind*.

If you ask the other John and Peggy (my parents) how they've managed to stay married for well over half a century, they'll credit an uncompromising level of honesty with each other. If you press them, though, you'll learn that their commitment to the truth did not extend to their children. Indeed, when it came to raising three boys on a public school teacher's salary, my parents lied like rugs.

I remember a television commercial that used to air during Baltimore Orioles home games. It was for an amusement park in Ocean City, Maryland. According to the announcer, a visit there would amount to "the time of my life." At that particular moment, my life had amounted to about nine years. For the most part, I was satisfied with the way things were going. Then I saw the Wild Mouse.

The Wild Mouse was a giant roller coaster that threatened to leap from our black-and-white television and smash through the wall of our tiny den. It shared the Ocean City boardwalk with the Round-Up, the Tilt-A-Whirl, and other mysterious contraptions that plunged and spun this way and that. I had never seen anything like them—a parade of machines devised for no purpose other than pure enjoyment. I remember the camera zooming in on a kid about my age. He was strapped into the Wild Mouse next to a pretty girl, his excitement teetering on the verge of rapture. I was transfixed.

"Hey, Peggy, get a load of these ding-a-lings on the TV. I think they're gonna puke on each other."

My parents were sitting on the sofa behind me. "Oh, those poor children," Mom said. "Why would anyone stand in line all day just to get vomited on?"

"Obviously, Peggy, those kids are deranged. Look at 'em."

I searched the sea of jubilant faces for signs of idiocy or nausea.

"Isn't it sad, John, how some children need machines to have fun?"

"It sure is, Peg. It sure is."

Later, another commercial appeared, this one for a movie called *Willie Wonka and the Chocolate Factory*. It was playing at the Senator and, according to the announcer, it was "a thrilling film for the whole family . . . a must-see event!" I had never been to the Senator before, or any other movie theater. I was captivated.

"Tell me something, Peg. Why would anyone want to see the movie when they could read the book instead? Books are so much more interesting."

"Well, John, as I understand it, movies are for children who can't read very well. Isn't that sad?"

"It sure is, Peg. It sure is."

In 1971, we didn't have the money for amusement parks or "must-see" events. But I never felt bad about missing such things. I was too busy feeling sorry for people who had to endure them.

"Hey, Dad, can we order a pizza tonight?"

"A what?"

We had never eaten a pizza before, much less ordered one. The concept of food delivery was completely foreign.

"Bobby Price says his mother has a pizza pie delivered right to their house every Friday night," I said. "And Chinese food every Wednesday."

My father sighed and spoke with a hint of sadness. "Look, son, Bobby's mother doesn't know how to cook. It's not her fault they can't have normal food." Then, quietly, to my mother, "Peg, maybe you should call Mrs. Price and give her the recipe for your meat loaf casserole."

"Of course, John. That poor boy deserves a home-cooked meal."

"He sure does, Peg. He sure does."

It was a strange sort of snobbery to develop at such an early age—this sympathy for the more fortunate—but that's precisely what my parents engendered. With duplicity and guile, they turned envy to pity. By the time I was eleven, I felt nothing but compassion for classmates of mine who had been forced to wear the latest fashions. Sadly, they had no older cousins to provide them with a superior wardrobe of "softer, sturdier, broken-in alternatives."

One Sunday after church, our neighbors came by with a slide-show from their most recent family vacation—hundreds of photos from Yellowstone and Yosemite. The Brannigans stayed for hours and hours and told stories about Indians and geysers and wild bears. My brothers and I were spellbound. When they left, my dad smiled and waved as they pulled out of the driveway, but when he turned around, his expression spoke for him: "Oh, those poor bastards," it said.

Like a Greek chorus of one, my mother dabbed at her eyes with a Kleenex. "Gosh, John, can you imagine flying all the way across the country just to take a walk in the woods?"

"No, honey, I sure can't. But then again, not everyone has a forest in their own backyard!"

"That's a good point, John. A very good point."

My parents shifted their gaze toward the large tract of woods just beyond our pasture and looked with satisfaction at the epicenter of the sensible, affordable amusements that kept my brothers and me occupied on a daily basis: a swift-running creek, a swamp of frogs and cattails, an old wooden bridge, and a maze of hidden trails that might lead anywhere.

Later, when I was less gullible (and TV commercials were more persuasive), a new parenting style would evolve: one that included phrases like "No!" and "Because I said so!" But when I entered the sixth grade, I did so with a firm understanding that movie theaters were for the illiterate, vacations for the unimaginative, and home delivery for lazy housewives who couldn't cook. As for amusement parks, they were probably okay, if you didn't mind waiting in line all day for the chance to vomit all over your friends.

ANOTHER TORTURED ARTIST

Back in the seventies, before the world knew him by a single name, a battered boy stared into an unforgiving mirror and considered his reflection: a split lip; a swollen jaw; a black eye. Painful, but not as painful as the words that accompanied the beating: "Look in that mirror, boy. Your lips are too fat for your mouth, your nose is too flat for your face, and your skin doesn't match your brothers'. I'm trying to run a business here!"

The boy in the mirror sighed. His father was right. His face was not the face of a pop star. It was a flawed face. A swarthy face. A face that he could no longer live with.

In his mother's makeup cabinet, the boy found a solution: a glass jar filled with white powder. He opened it, sprinkled some powder into his hands, and began to rub it onto his face, wincing as he did so. His wounds were still tender, courtesy of the man who wouldn't tolerate a single mistake onstage or even in rehearsal. But gradually the boy in the mirror saw his complexion lighten. Would it be enough to mollify his violent and unpredictable father? Would it be enough to satisfy the people who paid to see him perform?

Over time, as the boy's talent became more and more undeniable, those questions became less and less relevant. By the end of the seventies, the boy was famous. By the eighties, he was a national sensation. By the nineties, he was an international phenomenon. By the turn of the century, he was the undisputed King of Pop. But for all his popularity, he never stopped obsessing over the color of his skin. Even when his legacy was firmly in place. Even when his personal life began to unravel. Even when his unusual relationship with a fourteen-year-old boy led to scandal and a courtroom drama.

Even in the grip of depression and addiction, the King of Pop concealed his true complexion, right up to the day he died, alone in his bed.

If all this sounds vaguely familiar, perhaps it's because you know the story of another battered boy who stood before another unforgiving mirror—two centuries later, in the *nineteen*-seventies—and considered *his* reflection. His split lip, swollen jaw, and black eye. Painful, but not as painful as the words that had accompanied the beating: "Look at yourself, boy. Your lips are too fat for your mouth, your nose is too flat for your face, and your skin doesn't match your brothers'. I'm trying to run a business here!"

Funny how history so often repeats itself. Like his predecessor, the boy in *this* mirror was never comfortable with the source of his own reflection. He, too, was born with a skin tone that didn't match that of his brothers. He, too, was raised by a violent, unpredictable man who exploited his talent at every turn. And he, too, left behind a collection of popular music unlike anything the world had ever seen. But unlike his predecessor, *this* tortured artist lived in

the era of plastic surgery. If you google his name, you can see the evidence for yourself: a new nose, a new chin, new lips, new eyelids, another new nose, new cheekbones, new hair, another new nose, new eyebrows, new eyelashes, one more new nose—and through it all, a complexion that got lighter and lighter, right up to the day he died, alone in his bed.

It's tempting to blame the father for screwing up the son, and in this case perhaps we should. By all accounts, Joseph Jackson did a real number on the brilliant, deeply troubled artist we know by a single name—Michael. On the other hand, the old man did train and manage and shape the career of the most popular musician of our time. As did Johann, two centuries before.

Like Joseph, Johann forced *his* son to perform and rehearse every single day of his young life. Like Joseph, Johann relied upon his son to pay the bills. A son with a complexion that he felt was simply too dark.

Yet if you google *his* name, you'll find no visual evidence of his Moorish ancestry; no portraits that reflect his natural skin tone and no busts that reveal a single "non-German" feature. Thanks to a bottomless jar of white powder, Johann's son was able to keep his complexion a secret—one that the Nazis were happy to reinforce a hundred years after his death by insisting to the world that his unique musical genius was proof of German exceptionalism and a credit to the Aryan race.

Happily, the most tortured artist of all time never knew that his music would make it onto Hitler's playlist—a small blessing, perhaps, for the battered boy who was never comfortable in his own skin. The lonesome bachelor who never found his Immortal Beloved. The legendary composer who went deaf at the height of his powers, but kept on creating—even though he couldn't hear the applause his many masterpieces inspired. Such were the burdens of the original King of Pop, the man we remember today by a single name . . . Beethoven.

I was reminded of Beethoven the other day as I was flicking around the TV dial. It was a rainy Sunday in San Francisco, and I had just stumbled across Steven Spielberg's *Band of Brothers*.

Like *Caddyshack*, *Jaws*, and *The Shawshank Redemption*, *Band of Brothers* is something I can't not watch—and the scene I stumbled upon on this particular rainy Sunday is my favorite moment in the entire series. It's a scene I always rewind a few times, whenever I happen upon it. It's shot in one take with a Steadicam—which I find more than a little impressive. But the mood it evokes is what moves me.

The sequence begins in the wake of an Allied attack, with the old, shell-shocked citizens of a bombed-out German town walking like zombies through the rubble of their neighborhood, pulling their busted possessions out from massive piles of debris. As a small group of American GIs observe the tableau, we hear what might be the greatest piece of music ever composed: the sixth movement of Beethoven's Opus 131. It's not just a soundtrack for the scene, it's part of the scene itself. For nearly three minutes, four German men who have just lost their homes—an impromptu string quartet—stand in the ruins. As their countrymen pick through the rubble, they play this devastatingly beautiful movement—an amazing sequence that concludes when a GI opines, "I'll say this much for the Krauts. They sure know how to clean up."

"All you need is a little Mozart," another GI replies.

At which point Lieutenant Lewis Nixon, played flawlessly by Ron Livingston (the guy from *Office Space*), corrects the soldier with two lines delivered with a perfect blend of authority and world-weary wonder.

"That's not Mozart," he says. "That's *Beethoven*."

Why do I love this scene so much? In part, I think it's the juxta-position of beauty and destruction. Placed so closely together, each magnifies the other. The combination makes me weep every time I see it. I sympathize with the German civilians. But I *empathize*, deeply, with the GI who confuses Mozart with Beethoven. As someone who's publicly mistaken on a near-daily basis, I know the embarrassment of being corrected on camera. Indeed, when it comes to being corrected, you might say I *am* an expert.

On *Dirty Jobs*, I was corrected by hundreds of different bosses in every imaginable setting. As the perpetual new guy, I was corrected on windmills and oil derricks, coal mines and construction sites, frack tanks, pig farms, slime lines, and lumber mills. Today, I have a podcast that wades into history and biography and a Facebook page filled with legions of people determined to keep me honest. What I can tell you is, not much has changed. But I can also assure you: not all "correctors" are created equal.

Take my cantankerous field producer, David Barsky. Like my father, Barsky's incapable of listening to a story if some stray fact seems to be out of joint. Both men will interrupt a joke if they think it's being told the wrong way—or a lecture if they disagree with something the professor says. In fact, a few pages into this book, Barsky's going to read about Mel Brooks and call me—immediately, guaranteed.

"Hey, Genius," he'll say. "The 'vinyl' record you mentioned couldn't have been vinyl. It was shellac. It had to be, because vinyl wasn't being used for record manufacturing in 1944." This will be the highlight of Barsky's week.

My dad—a former history teacher—will call immediately to ask me how I knew that Custer's body was violated in the way I've described. "You don't know that!" he'll say. "Experts still argue about it!! Just because people claim it's the case, that doesn't make it so!!!" Those exclamation marks will be bouncing off satellites and entering my ears like arrows.

My mom is also a hopeless corrector—of the apologetic variety. At least, she pretends to be.

"Oh, Michael," she'll say. "I'm so sorry, but there's a double nega-tive at the top of this section. You said, 'I can't not watch.' Sorry, Mike, it's a great story, but I thought that you'd want to know."

Personally, I don't mind being corrected, even when I'm right. It's nice to know that people are paying attention. But when I am corrected, I prefer it to be in the style of Lieutenant Dixon. He didn't scold the GI for confusing Mozart with Beethoven. He wasn't haughty, pedantic, or disappointed. His words came with no apolo-gies, no exclamation points, and no attempt to lord his knowledge over his men. In fact, if you YouTube the scene, you'll see that he barely glances at the man he corrects. He simply rectifies the situa-tion definitively while remaining focused on the final few measures of Beethoven's movement.

By the way, I ran into Ron Livingston a few years ago in LA. He and some friends were eating sushi in a place called Katsu-Ya at a strip mall off Ventura Boulevard. I was a few tables away with my high school friend Chuck. Now, I've never approached a celebrity in my life—especially one with a mouthful of fish. But I couldn't help myself. I walked over to Ron's table and stood there quietly, making things awkward until he returned my gaze. I don't think Ron recog-nized me, but he did raise his eyebrows in the universal expression that means "What the hell do you want?" As his friends and my friend looked on, no doubt asking themselves the same question, I leaned in, paused for dramatic effect, and said, "All you need is a little Mozart."

For a moment, I thought he would leave me hanging. But he didn't. Lieutenant Dixon swallowed his fish, took a sip of his beer, and with barely a glance in my direction said precisely what I hoped he would say: "That's not Mozart. That's Beethoven."

Point is, the story that comes next doesn't include a single mis-take. But if you do find one, please drop by my Facebook page and tell me about it. And while you're there, say hello to my dad!!!

SIZE MATTERS

Bill had a big one, no doubt about it, but Craig's was bigger. Not by much, but in a contest where every inch mattered, Craig had more inches. So Bill made a few adjustments. Soon his was bigger than Craig's—at which point Craig made some adjustments of his own. Now Craig's was bigger than Bill's again and more interesting to look at—thanks to the enormous tip on the end. But Bill had one more trick up his sleeve. When the measuring finally stopped, one of these men could proudly claim to have the world's biggest erection.

When it comes to New York City architecture, size matters. No one knew that better than these two famous partners, who'd become bitter rivals in their quest to erect the Tallest Building in the World.

Their partnership had been legendary. Bill was the artist—a brilliant architect but mostly void of charisma. Craig was the consummate businessman—handsome, silver-tongued, and highly motivated. Together they had been a perfect team. Craig landed all the high-profile commissions. Bill designed the impressive, groundbreaking structures that made them both rich.

Unfortunately, their egos grew apace with their bank accounts. You see, Craig was an accomplished architect in his own right. He didn't appreciate the constant newspaper articles that raved about Bill's "artistic genius." And for his part, Bill resented being seen as the boardroom lightweight, incapable of handling big deals. He hated the way clients looked at Craig whenever they talked about money.

Eventually, the artist and the businessman went their separate ways in a very public, very nasty divorce. Then, as fate would have it, each one landed the commission of a lifetime.

In 1928, Bill was contacted by a business tycoon who wanted him to design the tallest building on Earth. Bill agreed and submitted plans for a soaring tower in Midtown Manhattan, 809 feet tall.

Shortly thereafter, Craig agreed to design the Bank of Manhattan Trust Building, down on Wall Street. According to his plan, he would build a grand tower, 840 feet in height.

Well . . . when Bill learned that Craig's design was thirty-one feet taller than his, he quickly added two extra floors to his blueprint. Craig responded by adding an extra floor to his. Bill followed suit.

Soon, both men were flirting with 900-foot designs. The public was transfixed. They watched as Craig gained the advantage. The base of his tower was broader than Bill's and could support more floors. Then Bill found a unique way to stretch his upper floors, adding extra height and dramatically altering the aesthetics in a way that no one had ever imagined.

When the final designs were approved, everyone assumed the battle was over: Bill's tower in Midtown would be the tallest building in the world. Craig's tower on Wall Street would be a close second. But a man like Craig could never be second banana, especially to his former partner. Both towers were completed in 1930. Then Craig whipped out his secret weapon: that giant tip, which he called the "Lantern"—along with a flagpole that brought 40 Wall Street to

927 feet—two feet taller than Bill's Midtown tower. 40 Wall Street was the tallest building in the world now, and Craig rejoiced in every glorious inch.

For about a month.

Because a man like Bill wouldn't be second banana, either—especially when his former partner was the man in the number one spot. Secretly, Bill had constructed a 185-foot spire, code-named the "Vertex." Its existence was known only to the small group of steelworkers who'd built the massive pinnacle and stored it in the building's elevator shaft. And so, on May 22—just thirty days after Craig laid claim to the world's biggest erection—Bill rode a private elevator to the seventy-first floor of his Midtown masterpiece. He looked out upon his former partner's looming behemoth, six miles to the south. Then he gave the signal. A giant crane hoisted the Vertex into place—making Bill's erection the biggest in the world and flipping his former partner the biggest middle finger ever raised over Manhattan.

Of course, erections are unpredictable things. Size matters, obviously, but by no means is it the only measure of satisfaction. Bill, for instance, in his haste to make his building bigger, overlooked something that Craig—the consummate businessman—would have never ignored: he forgot to get a signed contract with his client. Now the tycoon who had hired Bill to build a design he'd called "a monument to myself" was refusing to pay his full commission.

Bill took the tycoon to court. Eventually he got his money. But in those genteel days of boater hats and pocket fobs, a lawsuit was considered an ungentlemanly way to do business. By fighting over the size of his commission, this brilliant architect—Bill Van Alen—destroyed his own reputation. And even though his iconic tower is now considered by many to be the most significant structure ever to grace the Manhattan skyline, the tycoon who paid for it—Walter Chrysler—turned out to be his final client and the Chrysler Building his last public erection.

Unlike Bill the Artist, Craig the Businessman was well paid for his efforts at 40 Wall Street. His building is no longer the second tallest in the world, or the third, or the fifth, or the twenty-fifth. But it's worth remembering that, for one glorious month in the spring of 1930, nobody had a bigger one than H. Craig Severance—an architect who relished the art of the deal more than the artistry of his chosen trade.

Something, perhaps, for the current owner to reflect upon. Another New York builder who, from time to time, has ruminated upon the importance of size. A man whose last name now appears on the facade of 40 Wall Street in big gold letters. Enormous letters. Maybe the biggest letters in the whole world!

T-R-U-M-P

Okay: They might not be the biggest, but they're definitely . . . *yuge*.

Regarding erections, you know what they say: if it's not one thing, it's your mother.

In this case, my own. In *her* book, *About My Mother*, Peggy Rowe wrote unashamedly about her love for all things equine. As a teenage girl, she routinely slept in the barn, preferring the company of horses to people. According to my grandmother, she often missed meals and skipped school to dote on the ponies in her charge. Not much changed after she married my father and brought her three sons into the world. Our primary purpose, as best we could tell, was to pick up the endless piles of steaming manure that littered the modest pasture behind our farmhouse while she made sure that the horses were fed, watered, exercised, brushed, fed some more, brushed again, and tucked in for the night. Sometimes, after that, she would feed her children, but with far less enthusiasm.

When I was twelve, my mother entered me in an equestrian competition at the Maryland State Fair. She was determined to instill in me the same sickness that had infected her, and resistance was futile. "Mom," I said, "I don't want to ride English. It's for girls."

"Don't be ridiculous, Michael. The finest riders in the world ride English. Any fool can hang on to the horn and gallop around on western tack like a drunken cowboy."

That sounded good to me, far preferable to the navy blazer (with black piping) that I was compelled to wear, along with creamy spandex breeches, a blousy pirate shirt, and knee-high black boots. Worst of all was the helmet, a rounded bowl of a thing far too small for my already bulbous head, covered in smooth black velvet and held in place with an elastic chinstrap. I was so appalled by the thing, I could only stand there while Mom affixed it to my head.

I looked like a Pez dispenser on a pony. A pony named Tammy.

The competition didn't end well, the humiliation lingered, as humiliation often does, and to this day, I remain deeply suspicious of spandex, helmets, and females named Tammy. But those earlier memories have long since been eclipsed by a series of misadventures on various ranches and farms featured on *Dirty Jobs*. The first and, I suppose, the most memorable took place in Texas, with some assistance from a quarter horse called Paid by Chic—a beautiful creature whose ability to ejaculate on cue was far more humbling than falling off Tammy midway over the first jump had been.

Paid by Chic was led into the stable and brought to a pommel horse—a piece of gymnastic equipment whose name finally began to make sense. On the other side of the pommel horse, a mare in heat was waiting. Well accustomed to that daily dance, Paid by Chic was already . . . ready. My job was to approach the animal and guide his manhood—his horsehood, if you will—in all its vascular tumescence into an artificial vagina, thoughtfully presented to me by a veterinarian named Dr. Christine. The tumescence was humbling. The vagina was a bright blue container about the size of a bread box. Imagine a hot-water bottle with a heavy-duty fabric handle on the top. Dr. Christine handed me the device along with a tube of lubricant and a baby bottle.

"Go ahead," she said. "Squeeze some lube into the artificial vagina."

"How much?" I asked.

"Can't have too much lube," she said. "Now go ahead and screw that baby bottle into the back end."

"I beg your pardon?" I said.

"Plug up the back end of the artificial vagina with the baby bottle so the semen has somewhere to go. Just go ahead and screw it in."

In the long history of sentences I'd never heard before, that was another one. "Sooner would be better," she added.

Over on the pommel horse, Paid by Chic had assumed a position of pure, undeniable readiness. His front legs were draped over the side. His eyes were focused on the mare just out of reach. His horsehood was thrusting, pointlessly, into midair.

"Okay," I said. "I'm ready."

I approached the engorged beast.

"Hold on there, champion. You don't approach a horse in that condition without one of these. Last week, one of our best grooms got knocked unconscious."

Occupied as my hands were with a fully lubricated artificial vagina, augmented with a semen-catching baby bottle, I couldn't accept the yellow bicycle helmet Dr. Chris was offering me. I could only stand there, appalled, as she affixed it to my head. Like the velvet monstrosity from my youth, it didn't fit, even remotely. But once again I was in compliance and ready for action.

Moments after the episode aired, Mom called to congratulate me.

"Oh, Michael, you're so lucky! Paid by Chic is one of the greatest quarter horses alive! And you looked so handsome in your little bicycle helmet."

"Thanks, Mom. The whole thing was . . . humbling."

"Yes," she said. "I imagine it was."

I saw no need to mention that three minutes later, Paid by Chic had humbled me yet again with an encore performance. A performance that filled my baby bottle with another deposit of white gold. A performance worthy of all the close-ups, slow pans, and artistic dissolves that made *Dirty Jobs* the family-friendly show it was.

After all, she *is* my mother.

CAN YOU BE THERE BY NINE?

Al sat on the back of a horse that wasn't his, drew a pistol that wasn't loaded, and shot an Apache who wasn't an Indian. The stuntman screamed and fell unconvincingly to the ground, and the director yelled, "Cut! Back to one, everybody! Let's do it again!"

Al glanced nervously at his watch. 6:30 p.m. Not good. His audition was at nine the next morning—St. George, Utah, was seven hours from LA by car—and Al didn't have a car.

"All right, everybody, here we go. Ready? And . . . action!"

Once again Indians whooped and charged, townspeople screamed and scattered, and Al pulled the trigger, shooting the same guy for the tenth time that day. But now, when the Apache who wasn't an Indian fell to the ground, the director called, "Cut! That's a wrap, everyone! Check your call times for tomorrow!"

Al knew his call time already: 3:00 p.m. Tight but doable. He turned his horse away from the set of *Bullet for a Badman* and rode hard toward the nearest highway. It was rough terrain, but he could handle a horse. You probably knew that, if you'd seen him in *Springfield Rifle*, with Gary Cooper, *The Big Trees*, with Kirk Douglas, or

The True Story of Jesse James, with Robert Wagner. For a big man, he rode well.

Five miles later, as the sun was about to set, Al reached the highway. He dismounted, turned his horse back in the direction of the stables, and gave it a slap on the rump. One thing about horses: they always know where the stable is, especially around dinnertime. After that one left in a cloud of dust, Al knew that there was no turning back. He stuck his thumb out, and two hours later, an eighteen-wheeler finally pulled over.

"Where you headed, cowboy?"

"Los Angeles."

"I can take you as far as Vegas."

"I'll take it," said Al.

Al jumped into the cab. The truck driver said he looked familiar. Al asked him if he liked the movies.

"Sure," said the driver. "Who doesn't like the movies?"

"Did you see *Dive Bomber*, with Errol Flynn?"

"I don't think so."

"I was in that one."

"Oh, yeah? What else you been in?"

"Well, I was in *Up Periscope*, with James Garner."

"Didn't see it."

"*Time Out for Rhythm*, with Rudy Vallee?"

"Nope."

"What about *Rogue Cop*, with Rod Taylor?"

"Sorry."

"*To the Shores of Tripoli*, with Harry Morgan?"

"Negative."

"*The Sea Chase*, with John Wayne?"

"Uh-uh."

"*The West Point Story*, with James Cagney?"

"Doesn't ring any bells."

By the time they arrived in Vegas, it was firmly established that Al's driver was not up to speed with his passenger's résumé—but Al didn't mind. With a wife at home and four kids to feed, Al didn't care about being recognized. He just wanted to work. That's why he was busting his butt for a chance to audition for the role of Jonas Grumby, the final character to be cast on a new show for CBS. His agent said he looked like a Jonas Grumby, and Al couldn't disagree.

The driver dropped him at McCarran Field just in time to see the last flight to LA take off without him. Al slept in the terminal. The next morning, he boarded the first flight to Burbank, landing a half hour before his audition time, and grabbed a cab to the studio.

Al smiled when the cabbie picked up exactly where the truck driver had left off.

"You got one of those faces," said the cabbie. "Where have I seen you?"

"I dunno," said Al. "You like the movies?"

"Sure," said the cabbie. "Who doesn't like the movies?"

"Ever see *Monsieur Beaucaire*, with Bob Hope?"

"Don't think so," said the cabbie.

"I was in that one," said Al.

"Oh, yeah? What else you been in?"

Al sighed.

"*Home Town Story*, with Marilyn Monroe?"

"Didn't see it."

"How about *Battle Hymn*, with Rock Hudson?"

"Not yet."

"*No Time for Love*, with Claudette Colbert and Fred Mac-Murray?"

"It's on my list."

"*Young at Heart*, with Doris Day and Frank Sinatra?"

"Uh-uh."

Al arrived at the studio with two minutes to spare. He didn't look like a man who had ridden a horse, hitched a ride, and slept in an airport just for a chance to audition for a role he probably wouldn't get. Nor did he look like a man who would be flying back to Utah in less than an hour to shoot some more Apaches who weren't really Indians in another movie that no one would ever remember. He looked like a Jonas Grumby—the smiling, bumbling, exasperated character he'd come to read for.

Al glanced again at the lines, which he'd already memorized. He walked into the room. A skinny kid with a funny hat on was waiting in front of a camera. Al shook the kid's hand, and they chatted briefly about the scene. Then somebody said, "Action!"

That was that. Magic. No one would ever look at Al again and wonder where they'd seen his face. Thanks to that audition and five decades of syndication, Al's face would be forever seared into America's retina. Jonas Grumby would accumulate more screen time than all of the stars that Al had ever worked with combined.

And so when he died in 1990, Al's ashes were sprinkled over the Pacific Ocean—a fitting send-off for the man who became synonymous not with the cowboys he'd so often portrayed or the Indians he'd so often shot but with Jonas Grumby—the sailor whose name was changed, after the show's pilot, to the one you know today. The ubiquitous title by which he was called *every* day for the rest of his life.

Such was the fateful trip of Alan Hale, Jr., a great character actor who just happened to be an actor of great character. A man whose twelve-hour odyssey from St. George, Utah, to Los Angeles, California, earned him a three-hour tour to a deserted island that wasn't really deserted. An island where he was known as "The Skipper."

Even though the *real* boss was a skinny kid with a funny hat named . . . Gilligan.

Alan Hale, Jr., never won an Oscar or Emmy Award. He was never even nominated. But if Hollywood was in the business of recognizing character, surely there'd be a trophy somewhere with his name on it. Maybe even a statue. Because what Hale did back in 1964 was nothing short of heroic.

Imagine: You're a middle-aged character actor. You're not rich. You've got a wife and four kids, all of whom depend on you. In the middle of a paid gig in Utah, you sneak away on a horse that isn't yours and make your way to Los Angeles, on the off chance that you'll land a role you know nothing about. Then you get back to Utah in time to do the job you've already been hired to do.

Alan Hale, Jr., didn't give a damn about fame. He believed in something far more noble, something Hollywood has never recognized and probably never will. He believed that a promise made was a debt unpaid; specifically, the promise he'd made to care and provide for his family. *That's* what makes him a hero to me. And that's why his journey reminds me of another voyage by another actor . . . a regular guy who taught social studies for thirty years, started a vocational training program at the junior high school where he worked, raised three boys on a single income, and appeared in fifty productions of better-than-average community theater.

The first time I saw my dad onstage was in 1975, when he played the lead in a production of Woody Allen's *Don't Drink the Water*. That character was Walter Hollander, a middle-aged American tourist trapped with his family at the US Embassy in a fictitious country somewhere behind the Iron Curtain.

I was transfixed. Who was this man inhabiting my father's skin? Why was everyone laughing hysterically—not just at the things that he said but at the way he said them? Where was the no-nonsense teacher who'd come home every night and loom over me as I did homework? The stern taskmaster who woke me up every Saturday at 7:00 a.m. to split wood, mow the lawn, and shovel the snow?

Don't Drink the Water split my father's personality in two. He was still my father; still a dedicated teacher and church deacon; still the reliable head of our household. But every six months or so, he became an entirely new person: someone with bulging eyes and a funny accent. All that his wife and sons could do was watch the transformation, marvel, and take turns running lines with him.

I recall a production of Agatha Christie's *Towards Zero*. Dad played a Scottish inspector called in to investigate a murder at a country estate. From the front row, I watched him confront the guilty party with damning evidence. The expression on his face was one I recognized immediately: It was an expression that accompanied countless other investigations, all conducted in the house I had grown up in.

"And whose muddy boots left this dirt on the carpet?"

"And who drank the last of the milk?"

"And whose socks are these, jammed into the sofa cushions?"

Such questions, directed to my brothers and me, were always accompanied with a raised eyebrow and followed by some dramatic revelation: the muddy boot, empty milk carton, or wayward sock, held high for all to see: "A-ha!"

As a sleuth, he was a natural. My father's innate desire to get to the bottom of things informed his understanding of history and his desire to teach it to eighth graders as much as it drew him to plays that posed the question "Who done it?": *Dial M for Murder, Witness for the Prosecution, Twelve Angry Men, A Shot in the Dark, The Butler Did It, Deathtrap* . . . Dad's done them all. His portrayal of Judge Danforth in *The Crucible* comes back to me all the time.

"We burn a hot fire here; it melts down all concealment!"

Sitting in the front row at the Dundalk Community Theater, I was sure that his lines were directed at me—and seeing that there was more to my father than I had imagined made me wonder if, maybe, there was more to me? Mom certainly seemed to think so.

"One day, Michael, you'll be the star of the show. Just like your father."

If watching my dad was a privilege, working directly with him was an honor: a role you might say I was born for. In *The Rainmaker*, he played a sheriff who arrested me—for trying to convince desperate farmers I could make it rain during a drought. In *Inherit the Wind*, he played a judge (again) and threatened to send me to jail for contempt of court. That, too, was a very believable portrayal.

Seven years after Dad's debut in *Don't Drink the Water*, I appeared in a production of the same play. Not in the same role—I was still too young to play a middle-aged American tourist. I had auditioned for the part of Axel Magee, the hapless son of the US ambassador, who'd fallen in love with the beautiful daughter of Walter Hollander, the character my father had played.

The production was staged at the Cockpit in the Court—one of the more respected venues on the Baltimore theater scene. I had butterflies on opening night. I remember the audience murmuring on the other side of the curtain as the lights dimmed. But what I remember most clearly is Dad in the front row, laughing loudly in all the right spots, no doubt wondering "Who is this young man inhabiting my son's skin and getting all of these laughs?"

Coincidentally (or maybe not?) my dad was back at the Cockpit in the Court while I was writing my story about Alan Hale, Jr., auditioning for a role in another production of . . . you guessed it, *Don't Drink the Water*. Now that he was in his mid-eighties, he was too seasoned to play Walter Hollander. But thanks to a passable Russian accent and his no-nonsense demeanor, he did get cast in the role of Krojack, a KGB investigator determined to get to the bottom of things.

Watching from the front row, I thought about his many roles over the many years. All the rehearsing. All the time he's spent memorizing lines. I thought about the hospital he volunteers at two days a week and the shut-ins who anticipate his cheerful delivery of Meals on Wheels every Monday. I thought about the former students who stay in touch with him and the church that still relies upon him to collect and count the weekly offering. And I thought about the three boys he'd raised on a single income.

After the show, he told me that things weren't as easy as they used to be. But, as anyone who knows my dad understands, "easy" was never the point.

My guess is that Alan Hale, Jr., understood that as well.

A FULL-FIGURED GAL

Libby was a tall drink of water, no two ways about it. A statuesque, full-figured gal who was, in the words of Rodgers and Hammerstein, "broad where a broad should be broad." Beyond her classic beauty, though, Libby possessed another quality that most men found irresistible—a quality that suggested anything might be possible with a girl like her.

Fred had conceived Libby twenty years earlier—her mom had never really been in the picture—but it would be unfair to call Fred a single parent. Fred loved his girl as much as any father could love a daughter, but it was Gus who had actually raised her. And now Fred and Gus were trying to arrange a marriage, searching the world for a man who would put their girl on a pedestal.

For a time, it seemed that that man would be the governor of Egypt. Isma'il Pasha was handsome, charming, and clearly enamored of Libby. He said all the right things and promised to build her a fabulous home, right there at the entrance of the newly completed Suez Canal. Fred was delighted. Obviously, Isma'il was Muslim, but Libby didn't care about that. She'd wear the veil in public, if doing so would please him. But after two years of courtship, it became clear that Egypt was not the right place for a woman like Libby.

Libby took the rejection in stride, but Fred was beside himself. He had wasted two years with Isma'il, and his little girl wasn't getting any younger. So Fred and Libby sailed to America, to find a more suitable suitor. To everyone's surprise and delight, the mayor of Baltimore proposed. So did the mayors of Boston, Philadelphia, and San Francisco. American mayors seemed to have a thing for full-bodied gals who radiated possibility. But ultimately it was a Hungarian immigrant who persuaded Fred that New York City was the only sensible place for his daughter to call home.

At first glance, Joe was not an obvious match. He was a slender man who'd been described as "too scrawny for manual labor." Next

to Libby, he looked like a kid. But Joe knew exactly what he liked and precisely how to get it. Back in Missouri, as a reporter for the *St. Louis Post*, he had worked hard and saved his money. Eventually, he'd bought the entire newspaper. He'd bought the *St. Louis Dispatch*, as well. Then he'd moved to Manhattan and bought a newspaper called *The World*. New York was where Joe first laid eyes on Fred's daughter. That's when he proclaimed—on the front page of his new newspaper—that Libby would stay in the city with him.

Fred was delighted. Obviously Joe was a foreigner, but Libby didn't care about that. There was only one problem: when Fred told Joe that he and Gus wanted to see Libby on a pedestal, he wasn't talking in metaphors; he was talking about an actual pedestal—one that would cost the city of New York no less than $250,000. That's the equivalent of $6 million today.

Sadly, Joe didn't have that kind of cash lying around. But Joe was a man who knew exactly what he liked, and precisely how to get it. So, 150 years before crowdfunding became a thing, the journalist from Hungary turned his newspaper into a GoFundMe page and challenged his readers to keep Libby in New York City.

Philip and Eliza Bender were among the first to contribute, with 50 cents each. Joe printed their names, along with his thanks, right next to a photo of his beloved. Their kids pitched in, too, and Joe printed their names, as well: "Anna, 25 cents; Frannie, 25 cents; Leonard, 10 cents; Frank, 15 cents; Alice, 10 cents; Ralph, 10 cents; Carri, 10 cents; Miss Nicey, 25 cents." All in all, the Benders were good for $2.30—and everyone read all about it.

Soon hundreds of New Yorkers began donating their pocket change: street sweepers, carriage drivers, stonemasons, housewives, ordinary men and women with only pennies to spare. Anyone who donated saw his or her name in the newspaper, next to an image of Libby. Within months, the necessary funds were in hand, and soon after that, on a place called Bledsoe Island, the construction of a mighty pedestal began—a pedestal sturdy enough to support the full-figured gal that Joe was determined to keep in the Big Apple: the 450,000-pound, 151-foot statue called "Libertas."

Frédéric Bartholdi had conceived her and given her a name. Gustave Eiffel had raised her and given her a frame. But it was the immigrant from Hungary who'd given the lady from France a place to stand. Without Joe, Libby would be overlooking some other harbor. Philadelphia's, probably. Or maybe Baltimore's. Or, she'd be in some other country. She'd almost wound up behind a veil, at the mouth of the Suez Canal, dressed in the robes of an Egyptian peasant. Instead, she stands at the foot of Manhattan, where she welcomes the tired, the poor, the huddled masses yearning to breathe free.

It's funny: an immigrant, famous today for the prizes bestowed in his name, is largely forgotten for his greatest gift—the campaign that kept our favorite lady right where she belongs. Thanks to thousands of New Yorkers, their pocket change, and a man named Joseph Pulitzer, we can say that, once upon a time, America put Liberty on a pedestal.

———————————

I had a pedestal once. I put a pig on it. You can google it. Go ahead—I'll wait.

Are you back? Good. Let's continue.

By 2005, *Dirty Jobs* was an undeniable hit, but the network and I couldn't seem to agree on how best to promote it. They wanted a traditional marketing campaign with me at the center of it—a "working-class hero, earnestly attempting to master every blue-collar trade."

That made me very uncomfortable. *Dirty Jobs* was not an "earnest" show. Nor was it a show about me. It was a light-hearted tribute to real people who woke up clean and came home dirty. What I wanted was a campaign where everyday people were not only featured, but treated like stars. I imagined them dressed in their work clothes, as they appeared in the show, arriving in limos at a star-studded "red carpet" premiere—where they'd be swarmed by paparazzi and greeted by throngs of adoring fans.

Barsky—my intrepid field producer and partner in grime—wanted a campaign that featured me covered in "feces from every species" (a recurring theme in Season One). A stickler for realism, Barsky also proposed a campaign that featured intimate portraits of me with each of the barnyard animals I'd inseminated, artificially, in my ongoing attempts to demystify the secrets of animal husbandry.

All these ideas had one thing in common: they were non-starters. As a result, we were stuck. Happily, my lawyer was on the case.

I don't have an agent, or a manager, or a publicist. I have a Mary. Around the office, we call her the Irish Hammer.

Mary Sullivan is her full name. She's a former bio-major who woke up one day and decided to practice law instead. I'm glad she did. Mary has Farrah Fawcett's hair and Albert Einstein's brain, and once I realized the latter was bigger than the former, I started asking her opinion on everything.

Mary had caught wind of the "working-class hero" campaign already. She'd snorted, elegantly, and called my boss. "Mike isn't a hero," she had explained. "He's not the star of the show. He's not even a host. His job is not to be in the spotlight. His job is to shine the spotlight. My job is to keep him from becoming an asshole. Or worse, from looking like one."

Candor is a rare commodity in Hollywood. So, too, is charm. The Irish Hammer has both in spades, and so, the network had backed off. But now we were back to square one with the promo, and time was running out.

"What do you think I should do?" I asked Mary. "We need to film something this week."

Without looking up from her desk, the Irish Hammer said, "What about the pig?"

"What pig?"

"The pig in the show open."

Every episode of *Dirty Jobs* opens with a shot of me carrying a two-hundred-pound swine from a barn to a pigpen. (Incidentally, that pig appeared to have an erection, which nobody noticed until viewers started to write in with questions, but that's a story for another day.)

"I'm not sure I understand," I told Mary. "You want to make a pig the star of the show?"

"More like the mascot," she said. "A metaphor for hard work."

"But pigs don't work hard," I said. "Unless truffle hunting counts."

The Irish Hammer looked at me in the way that a smart person might regard an idiot.

"Do you know what a metaphor is?"

"I think so."

"Have you ever cleaned a pig pen?"

"Several," I said.

"Was it difficult?"

"Yes."

"Was it pleasant?"

"No."

"All right, then. If you want to honor people who do difficult, unpleasant jobs without coming off as earnest, or making it all about you, elevate the pig. Viewers aren't stupid. They'll figure it out. And you won't end up looking like an asshole."

See what I mean? Don't let the Farrah Fawcett hair fool you.

The next day we booked a three-hundred-pound sow for a most unusual photoshoot. She was chauffeured to Hollywood from a farm in Central Valley, and arrived in style at the soundstage bright and early, ready for her close-up. She was a perfect pig, straight from the animal equivalent of Central Casting: pink, with gray spots and a sweet disposition. Like Wilbur from *Charlotte's Web*, but all grown up. I called her "Rhonda."

In a pristine studio with white walls and a white floor, I watched as Rhonda was coaxed up a ramp that led to the top of a white pedestal, four feet off the ground. Once she was situated, the ramp was removed, and I took my place beside her. It was a simple setup. Standing next to Rhonda, I would look into the camera and riff about the unsung heroes of *Dirty Jobs*. I'd conclude with a pointed question: "So, what's on *your* pedestal?" It was a play on that credit card campaign: "What's in *your* wallet?"

I nailed it on the first take, in front of a roomful of nervous executives. Unfortunately, Rhonda nailed it, too. Just as I asked, "What's on *your* pedestal?" she crapped all over hers.

It was an enormous dump, delivered with impeccable timing. During the second take, Rhonda did it again, right on cue. This time, with a frightful spray of diarrhea that filled the studio with a sulfurous funk, blackening the white walls of our pristine set, and transforming my blue jeans into something browner. I could only marvel at the stench, while the horrified executives backed into a corner— a huddled mass, if you will, yearning to breathe free.

But Rhonda wasn't done. She crapped on every subsequent take, and when she could crap no more, she began to pee. She peed on my cameraman. She peed on her handler. She peed on me. Finally, when her bladder was empty, we got a take the network could use, along with a commercial that won several awards for "Excellence in Promos." (Yes, they have trophies for such things.) Interestingly, the footage that went viral was not the footage that aired, but the footage Mary encouraged me to release on YouTube after the fact. The outtakes of Rhonda at her incontinent finest. Those were hysterical, and viewed more times than the actual commercial. Go figure.

Looking back, putting a pig on a pedestal was maybe the smartest thing I ever did. Not only did it make Rhonda famous, it established me as the nontraditional host of a nontraditional show. One whose primary job was to appear more like a guest, and less like a host. And, whenever possible, not at all like an asshole. Opinions vary as to the degree to which I accomplished that, but I must have done something right, because Mary Sullivan eventually agreed to leave her firm and partner with me, for which I'm eternally grateful. And as for Rhonda, a poster of her now hangs in the office of the Irish Hammer. Like Libby, who welcomes the tired and the poor to these United States, Rhonda welcomes visitors to mikeroweWORKS, staring out from her pedestal, keeping me honest, and just a little bit dirty . . .

THE ORPHAN HERO

She was an orphan living on the cold streets of a hard town, doing what she had to do to get by. Unlike most runaways, she didn't bolt when they approached her. In fact, she greeted them with a curious smile and saw their government vehicle for what it was—a warm place on a cold evening. She got in.

Now, it's hardly a secret: orphans make great protagonists. Huck Finn and Harry Potter, Pip and Pollyanna, Dorothy Gale and Daenerys Targaryen—those characters stick with us. But their adventures are entirely fictional, while our protagonist is the real deal.

Twenty minutes after they found her, she was enjoying a hearty meal and a warm bath, both of which she needed. Then, for the first time in memory, she slumbered uninterrupted. When she awakened, she was escorted to a classroom, where she joined a handful of other recruits in various stages of the Program.

Our protagonist was a natural. Her instructors described her as "focused" and "a quick study." But it wasn't her aptitude that caught their attention; it was her demeanor. In every challenge, she remained unflappable, seemingly immune to the stress and fatigue that the

Program was designed to induce. Her instructors were impressed. On Halloween, just one week after they found her alone and freezing on the mean streets of the city, the decision was made.

They woke her up before dawn and led her to a small room. It was poorly insulated and impossibly cramped. She was seated on a drab leather cushion and commanded to remain as still as possible.

Wires, dangling from machines, were attached to her skin.

Food and water were left within easy reach.

Our protagonist remained calm. She asked no questions and offered nothing but that same curious smile before the men locked the door behind them.

Outside, the instructors gathered around a monitor and watched. Most recruits lasted fifteen or twenty minutes before the claustrophobia became too much to bear. She was different. Unfazed, she lay there for an hour, then another, then another after that—gazing calmly at the gray metal roof a foot above her head, smiling that same curious smile.

A day passed, then another. Finally, after three days locked inside the cold and gloomy enclosure, the wait was over. Buttons were pressed. Switches were flipped. The rumble of unfamiliar noises filled the air. Objects around her began to behave strangely, as the General Theory of Relativity became something more than a theory.

The sound around her intensified. So did her speed. Within moments, she was hurtling through the troposphere, the stratosphere, the mesosphere, the thermosphere, entering space at 18,000 miles per hour. She was an orphan, 4,000 miles above the streets she used to wander—the first of her kind to orbit the Earth.

Those of you who remember the very first days of the space race might recall the way the world held its breath, praying for her safe return. Our protagonist circled the earth four times in zero gravity as the scientists far below monitored her vitals, duly recording every precious scrap of data, until there was nothing left to record. Sputnik II would carry her corpse another 2,566 orbits before plummeting to Earth, leaving no remains for a proper funeral.

Her name was Laika, and though she was most certainly female, she was not a woman. She was a trusting terrier with a curious smile, a patient disposition, and ears that bent in several directions at once. You see, the Soviets recruited their very first cosmonaut from the frigid streets of Moscow because they needed a hardy specimen— a cadet who could endure the cold of a poorly insulated capsule. In other words, they needed a dog with the right stuff.

Today, Laika's sacrifice is well known in Moscow. In fact, if you visit the icy capital of the former Soviet Union, you'll see her there, back on the streets she used to wander. Memorialized in bronze, she stands upon a rocket and looks toward the heavens—an eternal reminder to those on two legs that "one small step for man" was made possible by one giant leap by . . . man's best friend.

Full disclosure: That last story almost broke me. It was the first one I wrote for *The Way I Heard It*, and it generated more sad-faced emojis and disappointed emails than any of the others. It also inspired an angry voice mail from my mother.

"Michael. What the hell is wrong with you? No one wants to hear a story about a puppy who dies in outer space! Now I'm depressed, damn it. And using bad language. Call me back."

Interesting. I've written lots of stories about man's inhumanity to man, but that was the one story that upset my mother. My girlfriend, Sandy, didn't take it well, either. At the end of Laika's sad tale, she threw her headphones across the room.

"The Russians built her a statue?" she said. "Who cares? Those godless bastards sent her into space for seven days with just one meal? What a bunch of cold-blooded scumbags."

Sandy struggles sometimes to say how she really feels. Like when Michael Vick was convicted of running a dog-fighting ring. "That guy should be fed to the tigers," she said.

"The Detroit Tigers?" I asked.

"No, just regular tigers. The NFL could sell tickets. They'd make a killing."

I don't have much sympathy for Michael Vick, either. But it's striking: people seemed to feel more strongly about his dogs than they did about the homeless people they had to step over on the way to their local sports bar. Were those people simply overwhelmed by the sheer volume of human suffering in the world? It's easy, these days, to turn on CNN, pick up the paper, or scroll through your news feed and conclude that the world's gone to hell. Maybe it has. But is it really worse than it's ever been? I don't think so. We're *exposed* to more bad news than ever before, and I think we lack the bandwidth to process so much misery. As Joseph Stalin said—and he would have known—the death of one man is a tragedy; the death of one million is a statistic.

Is that why the story of one little dog—who died alone, with her little heart racing, way out in space—cut so deeply?

The truth is, I didn't sit down to write about Laika just because I disapproved of the way she was treated. Nor did I write about her to provoke my mother into a fit of profanity; that was just a bonus. I wrote about Laika because, once upon a time, she brought the whole world together. And if I'm being *entirely* honest, I wrote about her because she reminded me of another fifteen-pound terrier mix—specifically, the one chewing on my slippers right now. The one Sandy plucked from a pound in Marin and brought to our apartment in San Francisco.

When he came to me—nameless and friendless and tiny and cold—I did what I often do in moments of great uncertainty: I went to my Facebook page and asked people who "like" me to name him. Those are the same people who have been programming every show I've worked on since *Dirty Jobs*. The same people who have suggested many of the subjects I've written about in this book. I like them, too, and I've come to believe that their collective opinion is perilous to ignore. So I posted a few photos of my new dependent and watched in wonder as eighty-seven thousand people wrote in with their suggestions.

It was an amazing thing to behold: my little mutt had the whole Internet by the tail.

After much consideration and some decidedly nonscientific methodologies, I selected the six most popular names. I unfolded a pee pad with six squares on it and wrote one name on each square. Then I set up a camera and waited for my puppy to poop, assuring my Facebook followers that I'd name him according to whatever name he pooped upon. Coincidentally (or maybe not?) the puppy pooped on "Freddy"—the name of my beloved high school teacher and mentor. What were the odds? One in six, I suppose. Looking back, though, it feels inevitable.

Point is, in 1957, an orphan from the mean streets of Moscow went to space—and the whole world watched, holding its breath, praying for her safe return. Sixty years later, an orphan from the mean streets of Marin took a dump—and 87,000 people watched, with baited breath, to see where that dump would land. Yet only one is remembered today as a hero.

"Give me a break," Sandy's saying. "Laika's no hero. She didn't *decide* to be shot into space, any more than Freddy decided to be videotaped crapping. That statue was built by assholes with a guilty conscience. Period. End of story."

She's right. Turning Laika into a hero was a fine way for the Russians to control the narrative. I suppose I control Freddy's narrative—which is why there's no statue in his future. I don't think he'd want one anyway: he seems happy enough with his bone, my slippers, and his own ghostwritten blog. There's even talk of a book deal, God help us. But if there *were* a statue, I know precisely what it would look like: Freddy in bronze, the pee pad in bronze, and a pile of bronze poop partially covering his name.

Now, that's a statue I could get behind.

SOMETHING IS MISSING

A young officer in a pivotal battle—exasperated by the indecision of his general—takes matters into his own hands. Leaping astride his trusty steed, he gallops to the front of the line to rally his troops. From the back of his horse he laughs at the enemy, ignores the bullets that fly past his head, and addresses his men like Henry V at Agincourt. According to the many firsthand accounts, it was a moment worthy of a monument.

"He was suddenly in the front of the line," said one soldier, "his eyes flashing, pointing with his saber to the advancing foe, with a voice that rang clear as a trumpet."

"He came from nowhere," another said, "and electrified the men. He simply willed us to follow him, and so we did."

In a totally audacious maneuver, the young officer led three thousand men straight into the flank of a superior foe, scattering the enemy and allowing his general to march his remaining force straight across the battlefield and win the day. But alas: something was missing. Namely, the general's remaining force.

Incredibly, the general had been worried about the wrong thing: Who would end up getting credit for this victory? And so he'd withdrawn his remaining men, settling for a draw. In the official battle report, the general acknowledged the gallantry of those three thousand soldiers, but again something was missing: the name of the brave young officer who'd led the charge.

Three weeks later, when both sides clashed on the same bloody fields, it was déjà vu all over again: at the pivotal moment, the general hesitated, and once again, the ambitious young officer leapt upon his trusty steed and rode to the front lines—this time in direct defiance of his furious commander. When he reached the front line, he reared back on his horse. Once more he shouted to the troops, "Hello, old friends! So good to see you again. What say you? Shall we win the day once and for all? Shall we send these bastards back across the sea?"

In the movie version, this is where the slow motion begins. The cacophony of battle drops away, replaced by soaring strings. Musket balls and grapeshot whir past our hero's head as a junior officer falls in a bloody heap beside him. The strings fade as we hear his pumping heart and labored breath. Close-up on his left leg: the same leg that's been twice wounded in earlier battles. A musket ball has lodged deep in his thigh. His temples pound as white-hot pain cascades through his body. Still our hero rides on. Another musket crack, and all is silent as a gaping wound in his horse's neck spews a crimson river. The great beast howls, rears back, and collapses on our hero, shattering his wounded left leg.

Fade to black.

There are rare moments that turn the tide of every battle, rare battles that turn the tide of every war, rare wars that turn the tide of human history. That was one of those moments in one of those battles in one of those wars. As in the Battle of Hastings in 1066, when William, Duke of Normandy, conquered England. As in the Battle of Orléans in 1429, when Joan of Arc saved France. As in

D-Day in 1944, when Dwight D. Eisenhower directed the Allied advance into Normandy. The heroes of those battles were recognized for their valor. One became a king, one a saint, one a president. All were honored with statues that stand to this day.

So, too, was the young officer with the shattered leg who lay beneath his horse 240 years ago. Indeed, on that very spot on this very day, you can still see the monument to our hero, erected a hundred years after his glorious charge, carved in granite to last through the ages. The inscription on the back spells out the magnitude of his contribution: "In memory of 'the most brilliant soldier' of the Continental Army, who was desperately wounded on this spot . . . winning for his countrymen the Decisive Battle of the American Revolution."

That's high praise. But it's curious—if you visit this monument for yourself, you might notice that something . . . is missing. For starters, the hero's gaze. His eyes are not overlooking the Hudson Valley in triumph, as you might expect them to be—because his statue has no head. His left hand does not hold the reins of his trusty steed, and his right hand does not point a gleaming saber toward the enemy—because his statue has no arms. Closer inspection reveals that something else is missing: shoulders, along with hips and a torso. The legs are conspicuously absent. Even the trusty steed to which the aforementioned reins might be attached is nowhere to be found. Indeed, there is nothing to this monument but a left boot, draped unceremoniously over the muzzle of a cannon.

And then you understand why. The young officer memorialized in such a strange fashion forgot to do something on that fateful day—he forgot to die. Pity. Had he simply bled to death in the mud underneath his horse, he'd have cities and schools named in his honor today, along with a proper statue that included his horse, his saber, and the rest of his body.

But alas, our hero not only survived the battle, he refused to let the surgeons amputate his ruined limb. His ego would not permit it. He spent the rest of his life in constant pain, hobbling around on a left leg three inches shorter than the right while completely neglecting the less obvious injury that would fester in ways that no doctor could treat: the wound to his pride, which went on to destroy the only thing he valued more than his life.

You may not remember Horatio Gates, the indecisive American general who squandered multiple opportunities to defeat the British. But I bet you'll remember the name of his young officer—the soldier whose bold action won the decisive battle that convinced the French to join America's fight for independence—a decision that, according to the French, anyway, turned thirteen unruly colonies into the United States of America.

Who knows? Had General Gates simply acknowledged the uncommon valor of his young officer, rather than hoarding all the credit for himself, our hero might have made some different choices after his injuries at Saratoga. Maybe then he'd have gotten a proper monument.

Instead, he got The Boot—the only statue ever dedicated to a specific war hero where something remarkable is missing: the hero's name; in this case, the name of a young officer whose courage helped free a nation, but whose pride turned his once good name into the very definition of betrayal . . . Benedict Arnold.

In 2002, an artist in Oakland offered to cast me in bronze, free of charge. Though it was tempting to think otherwise, his generous offer had nothing to do with me and everything to do with free publicity. It was the kind of quid pro quo to which I'd become accustomed as the host of a long-running, inexplicably popular TV show in San Francisco.

According to *TV Guide*, *Evening Magazine* provided a half hour of "human interest stories and local color." For the most part, this was true. *Evening Magazine* was packed with segments about local artists, Napa Valley getaways, hidden Bay Area gems, quirky collectors, ingenious inventors, and the kind of people who see the Virgin Mary in their French toast. If there was a three-legged dog in Marin, struggling to overcome canine-kidney failure, or a grape-stomping contest at the State Fair, you could count on *Evening* to bring you the story.

As one of the hosts, my job was to introduce these squishy little segments from a different location each night—usually a five-star spa, a museum opening, or the latest Michelin-rated restaurant in Nob Hill. Not exactly meaningful work, but I was good at it, and happy to assume the many perks that came with being a local celebrity. For instance, the artist who reached out to me knew that the promotional value of appearing on a segment was much greater than the $15,000 he'd typically charge to cast a B-list celebrity in bronze. He also knew that a B-list celebrity would find the prospect of preserving his enormous head for posterity too tempting to ignore. Like Alan Hale, Jr., I had not won an Emmy—an unforgivable oversight in a world where everyone is entitled to their own trophy. Perhaps a bronze bust of my chiseled visage could fill the void?

My cameraman and I drove to the artist's studio in Oakland. There, I sat for dozens of photos, each taken from a slightly different angle, until every square centimeter of my giant cranium had been captured. Based on those photos, and with the help of some mysterious software program, we made the initial mold, as well as the negative. Several weeks later we returned and filmed me pouring bronze into the negative. Then we returned once again and revealed the finished product.

It was a win for everybody. Viewers got an entertaining look at an intriguing process. The artist was flooded with requests from other narcissists, all of them happy to pay $15,000 for a permanent reminder of their favorite subject. And I got my long-overdue trophy: a three-dimensional, two-hundred-pound selfie.

My delight was short-lived, however. Where, exactly, does one display a two-hundred-pound version of one's own head? In the entryway? On the piano? Atop the mantel? Sandy and I lived in a modest apartment—one too small, it seemed, for this oversized doppelgänger. "It's too heavy for the mantel," she said. "And we don't have a piano. Or an entryway. Plus I don't like the way it looks at me." Sensing my disappointment, she added, "Maybe I'll feel differently after you're dead?"

She had a point. Statues and busts weren't meant to be seen by the subjects they honor, just as photographs weren't meant to be taken by the people who are in them. But what's the appropriate waiting period, after my demise? A month? A decade? These days, statues are being pulled down right and left. Perhaps if we'd waited a bit before building monuments to people we think we admire, we wouldn't be tearing those same monuments down today?

Think about it: It took us a hundred years to give Benedict Arnold his monument. That gave multiple generations plenty of time to consider the depth of his treachery, as well as his valor on that particular field. As a result, he got the memorial he deserved—one that has yet to be toppled. But if Sandy's right, and animal lovers realize the Russians built their statue to Laika not to honor her but to cover their own, conniving asses, should they reconsider that statue ? What about Lady Liberty, who seems a bit wobbly up there these days, on that magnificent pedestal of hers?

Thinking about it's not going to stop me from filling my Facebook page with selfies. (Those little monuments are impossible to topple!) But I assure you, today, "Bronze Mike" sits right where he belongs—under a tarp in my garage, next to some firewood and a bike with two flat tires. He's been there for years, out of sight, out of mind, dreaming of the day that he might emerge from the shadows to share the limelight with another monument: one that I'm in no great hurry to accept. The only monument everyone gets. The granite monument inscribed with the words we hope will sum us up, even as they let us down.

WORDS, WORDS, WORDS

George understood the consequences of words better than most. So did his son. But now, staring dumbly at the blank tombstone that would mark his boy's final resting place, George was at a loss to find the right ones. What words could possibly sum up the life of the poet that millions of people all over the world were now mourning? "Loving son"? That wouldn't work. "Beloved husband and father"? Hardly.

In the end, George went with "*Kata ton daimona eaytoy.*" "True to his own spirit."

George was satisfied with those words. He hoped James would have approved. But, truth be told, approval was not something George had ever received from James. Nor in fairness, was it something George had ever offered his rebellious son. Indeed, father and son hadn't spoken since the fateful day James had told the old man he was joining a band.

"A band? What kind of band?"

"A rock-and-roll band. I'm going to be the singer."

"That's ridiculous," George had scoffed. "Rock and roll isn't music. Besides, you can't even sing."

Now, looking down upon the granite bust of the young man with the long hair and the unearthly gaze, he contemplated the magnitude of his mistaken assessment. George thought about the thousands of protesters who'd been galvanized by his son's words and music. He also thought about some *other* words—ones that he'd spoken in haste six years earlier.

Back then, George had been patrolling a tense and danger-ous coastline in a place most Americans had never even heard of. The seas were high that evening, the fog was thick, and the radar screen showed enemy ships approaching from several directions—

approaching quickly. They didn't respond to any warning or communication, so George did what he had to do: speaking the words that would change history, he said, "Open fire!"

Those words went down to the gunners, men who—unlike George's son—were not inclined to ignore his orders. For nearly four hours, George's navy fired upon enemy ships that refused to leave his radar screen.

Meanwhile, thousands of miles away in Washington, DC, President Johnson got word of the sea battle. He interrupted all three of the networks with some words of his own: "This new act of aggression on the high seas must be met with a positive reply."

On national television, the president asked for and received congressional approval to retaliate, and the Gulf of Tonkin Resolution was passed. Back in the gulf, though, after the fog of war had finally lifted, George saw why the enemy ships had been unsinkable: they weren't actually there. The radar hits were not ships at all. They were anomalies brought about by bad weather and high seas, or maybe a technical glitch. Whatever the cause, George had been firing into a ghost fleet.

George reported the error to his commanders in Hawaii. They called McNamara immediately, but the secretary of defense—for whatever reason—didn't relay the message to the president. The air strikes went off as scheduled and, just like that, we were at war with Vietnam.

Yes, George understood the consequences of words.

Spoken in anger, they had divided his family. Spoken in error, they had divided his country. People still argue about whether his words were an honest mistake or part of a government conspiracy to push Congress into declaring a premature and completely avoidable war. Perhaps the answer to that is best addressed by the words of his son, who once wrote, "There are things known and things unknown, and in between are the doors."

Fitting words, from a rebellious boy who remained true to his own spirit. The son who could sing after all, and proved it, by providing a soundtrack to the war his father had started. A dead poet named . . . Jim Morrison.

It was Saturday morning. I was fourteen, and there was my father, standing at the foot of my bed, sharpening a double-sided ax.

"It's time," he said. "Let's go."

My father has a tendency to start conversations in the middle of sentences. He's also suspicious of anything modern—like nouns.

"Time for what?"

I knew the question was futile before I had asked it. So as I rolled out of bed and pulled on my jeans and my work boots, I tried another one: "Is it cold out?"

"Invigorating," he said. "Your mother made oatmeal. Eat fast."

Our Massey Ferguson tractor idled outside as we loaded up our wooden cart: ropes and pulleys, jacks and wedges, two chain saws, and various other weapons of war. Mom added a lunch box filled with ham sandwiches and green apples to our arsenal, along with a large thermos of coffee. It was snowing already.

"Try not to kill yourselves," she said. "Dinner's at six."

I can't count the number of times that my dad and I drove the old tractor down that stone road. We'd go through the lower pasture and deep into the woods to do battle with the Pine, the Maple, the Oak, and (his favorite) the mighty Locust.

"The hard wood puts up a tough fight, but it burns the best," he would say. The fact that we heated most of the old farmhouse with nothing but a wood stove was a source of great pride for my father and endless inspiration for witticisms like "Chop your own wood—it'll warm you twice!"

The man took great pleasure in finding just the right tree. What he loved even more was chopping that tree down. Although there was nothing nearby but the ground for the tree to fall on, he liked to pretend that there was. He imagined himself as the contestant on some sort of lumberjack game show—challenged, perhaps, to drop the tree between a Mercedes and a school bus full of children, with nothing but inches to spare on each side. With pulleys and ropes and lots of delicate chain-saw work, he would coax the tree to the ground, determined to see it land precisely in the spot where he wanted it.

Once that was done, we'd strip the limbs and the branches and cut them down to stove-length pieces. Then we'd turn our attention to the trunk, working backward from the top of the tree to the bottom. As the cuts became progressively thicker, the chain saw whined louder and higher.

"Sharpen that blade, son! A dull one's twice as dangerous!"

I still remember how my arms shook, even after the saw had been turned off and stowed away.

Hauling all that wood back to the house was a full day's work, but splitting the larger chunks into smaller pieces that would fit into our insatiable wood stove—that was a chore without end. Every day after school meant an hour up in the woodpile with Dad. I can still hear his voice as I got ready to swing the ax: "Aim for the chopping block, son, not the wood. If you aim for the wood, you'll hit nothing."

A smart man named Einstein once said, "People love chopping wood. In this activity one immediately sees results."

Being Einstein, he was right: chopping wood *does* yield immediate results—it's immensely gratifying just watching the progress unfold. But up there in the woodpile, the gratification was always delayed. Delayed because my father wasn't just teaching me how to swing that old double-sided ax—he was teaching me that work and play were two sides of the same coin. He was showing me that hard things—challenging things—could also be fun. In fact, the challenge was where the fun was.

Today I wonder: Did the Morrisons have a woodpile behind their house? Some place where George could show Jim that there were dangers involved when it came to cutting against the grain? A place to illustrate the consequences of driving wedges too deeply into the stubbornest stumps? What I know from personal experience is that fathers and sons *can* find the right words. They can find them in the woods when they go there together to get the fuel that they need to keep their family warm.

CALL IT WHAT YOU WILL

Peter stood dumbstruck in the doorway of his bathroom, searching for just the right word. "Ghastly" came to mind, followed in no particular order by "grisly," "gruesome," and "graphic." There on the bathroom floor, sitting in a puddle of his own blood, was Peter's uncle, Sir Samuel Romilly. Moments earlier, the two men had been in the study, going over the "Treasure House" Peter had been working on. Then Sir Samuel had risen from the couch, walked into the bathroom, picked up a straight razor, and dragged the blade across his throat.

"Dear God," cried Peter, as he ran to Sir Samuel's side. "What have you done?"

The answer was self-evident: Samuel Romilly had severed his carotid artery, along with his windpipe. Heartbroken by the death of his beloved wife—which had occurred three days earlier—the poor man had entered a state of bottomless grief. Or was it something more than grief? Despair, perhaps? Devastation? Despondency?

Call it what you will, the mental anguish had been more than Sir Samuel had been able to bear, and Peter could only watch as his uncle tried to scribble his final thoughts onto a piece of bloody stationery.

"My dear," he wrote, "I wish . . ."

He couldn't find the right words. He sat there instead, staring at the blank page, bleeding all over the bathroom floor. Moments later, he died in his nephew's arms.

Peter was no longer dumbstruck. He'd moved on to traumatized. Nonplussed. Astonished. Gobsmacked, he did what he always did when the chaos of an unpredictable world threatened to overwhelm him. He walked back to his study, opened his Treasure House, and started writing.

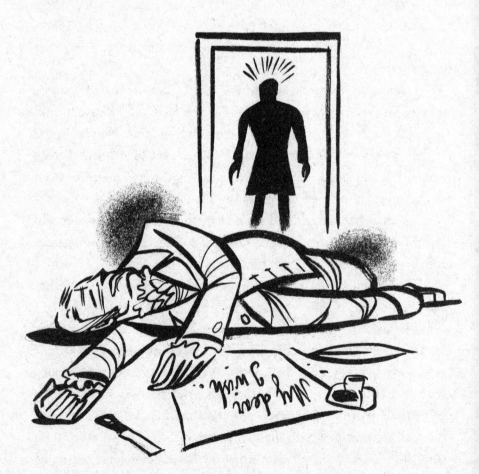

* * *

Two years later, sitting alone in the gloom of his parlor, Peter was once again searching for just the right word. Was he depressed? Probably. With a schizophrenic grandmother, a paranoid mother, a bipolar sister, an overly anxious daughter, and, of course, a suicidal uncle, Peter knew that melancholia ran in the family. But to what degree was he afflicted? Was he disheartened or merely down in the dumps? Was he disenchanted? Dismayed? Or demoralized? Would he succumb to the same darkness that had claimed his uncle?

Call it what you will, but as Peter pondered the precise nature of his malaise, his ennui, his languor and lugubriousity, he couldn't help but notice that the wheels on the carriages passing by his window appeared to be breaking the laws of physics. At least that's how they looked through the slats of his partially opened shutters. Interesting. After much observation and careful thought, he concluded that his eyes were retaining an image of the spokes for a fraction of a second after the slats in the shutters had interrupted the rotation of the wheel, thereby creating the illusion that the spokes were moving backward. Hmmm. That wasn't just "interesting"; it was intriguing. Titillating. Maybe even . . . beguiling?

Call it what you will, Peter was definitely onto something. So, once again, he reached for his Treasure House, which was considerably thicker than it had been two years earlier. He began to write a detailed analysis of what he'd just observed. He called it "Explanation of an Optical Deception in the Appearance of the Spokes of a Wheel Seen Through Vertical Apertures."

It wasn't exactly the title of a best seller, but then, Peter wasn't writing one. He was just trying to make sense of the chaos in an unpredictable world. The result? Hundreds of scholarly papers on countless natural phenomena, in this case, a detailed explanation of the defect in the human retina that came to be known as "persistence of vision"—a principle that explains the illusion of motion. A principle that led Peter to fabricate a prototype. A prototype with a shutter similar to the shutter that hung in Peter's parlor and an aperture similar to the window from which his shutter hung.

Now, I could just say, "That's the way I heard it"—and direct your attention to Tinseltown, where the name of the man most responsible for creating the motion picture camera is honored today with a star on the Hollywood Walk of Fame. I could, but I won't, because ironically, or perhaps paradoxically—or better yet unjustly—Peter's name isn't there.

Nor is it in the halls of NASA, even though Peter invented the slide rule—a mathematical breakthrough that enabled us to get a man on the moon.

Nor is it on the aquifers of London—even though Peter did find a way to purify England's drinking water.

Nor is it on the facades of hospitals—even though Peter was primarily responsible for the development of general anesthesia.

Peter's name isn't on the cover of the *Encyclopaedia Britannica*, though hundreds of scholarly papers he wrote, on countless natural phenomena, can be found therein: no fewer than 300,000 words written by Peter—words that helped explain the chaos of an unpredictable world.

The point is, we don't remember this prodigy, this polymath, this pansophic, for his incredible list of accomplishments; we remember him for his incredible list of words. Specifically, the list of words he compulsively compiled to combat the depression that perpetually plagued him. Words whose early assemblage began as a unique form of therapy but whose ultimate congregation went on to become an eponymous compilation of rhetorical replacements that went on to sell no less than 40 million copies over the next two centuries.

I refer, of course, to the indispensable directory of dialectical determination that was destined to dramatically increase the word count of every term paper that's ever been written, authored, or penned, while helping millions of aspiring writers prove conclusively that "alliteration almost always annoys." I'm talking about an unparalleled linguistic lineup of syntactical substitutes; a crucial compendium of etymological options; a singular source of all things synonymous, conceived in serendipity and dedicated to the proposition that no crossword puzzle should ever go unfinished.

Call it what you will: that tome on your bookshelf wouldn't be there today but for the grief-stricken uncle who died searching for the right words—and the melancholy nephew who never stopped collecting them.

A remarkable collection that Peter Roget called his "Treasure House." Or, if you prefer Latin . . . his *Thesaurus.*

A while ago now, on a flight to Baltimore—the same flight I'm on now, in fact—I stumbled across an *Atlantic* article about Roget. It was not what you'd call complimentary.

The article was written by Simon Winchester, who's worked on various documentaries for the History and Discovery channels; I've had the pleasure of narrating a few. Winchester wrote a terrific book, too, about the making of the Oxford English Dictionary: *The Professor and the Madman.* I'd recommend it. In fact, I just did. But I was surprised to find that, putting it mildly—or gently or reticently—Winchester wasn't a fan of *Roget's Thesaurus.* In Winchester's view, Roget did more to discourage good writing than encourage it. According to the *Atlantic,* "good writing" has little to do with finding the right word and everything to do with "the brave employment of the words that one already knows."

"Our literary powers are born," Winchester wrote, "not out of banal and mediocre suggestion, not out of lexical shopping lists, but out of passion, thought, and intensity of feeling."

Is Winchester right? Beats me. With or without Roget's help, I wouldn't know how to write novels. I wouldn't know where to begin.

But I do write these stories and, from time to time, I must confess, my search for *le mot juste* compels me to consult the innumerable and countless, multitudinous and myriad, infinite, incalculable, and unnumbered possibilities that *Roget's* affords. In fact, I did—when I wrote Roget's story. Which begs the question, was the tale really diminished—lessened, minimized, or smallened in some way—when I started to lean on that linguistic crutch? What about my captain up there, in the cockpit. Is he cheating me out of an honest flight by relying on the autopilot? By the same token, did I cheat on my taxes this year by relying on the succor and support of a little machine I call the "calculator"?

Whatever the answers are, good on you, Simon, for protecting the integrity, the probity, and the sanctity of the writer's craft and profession. But let's hear it, too, for those who have pulled themselves up by their own intellectual bootstraps while conceding that sometimes it's okay to just ask for some help.

NOT YOUR
TYPICAL HOMEMAKER

Julia stepped out of her tent after dawn and marveled at the sight in front of her: a sloping hill covered with wildflowers, a pristine beach, an unlimited view. Bill was a catch, no doubt about it: handsome, successful, ambitious. His proposal had taken her by surprise. But having slept on the idea, Julia was still undecided. Bill was the kind of guy who believed a man's home was his castle, which begged the question: Did he see himself as a king? If so, what did that make her? Bill's happy little homemaker?

Coincidentally (or maybe not?) Julia held in her hands a copy of yesterday's *San Francisco Examiner*, which Bill had left on her suitcase. On the front page, just below the fold, was an article entitled "Rules and Advice for Wives." It wasn't really an article; it was more like a public service announcement, printed for the edification of America's aspiring homemakers. Did he intend for her to see those rules before he popped the question? Julia didn't know, but she perused them nevertheless.

1. Don't be extravagant. Nothing appeals more strongly to a man than the prospect of economic independence.

2. Keep your home clean. Nothing is more refreshing to the eyes of the tired, nerve-racked worker than the sight of a well-tidied home.

3. Do not permit your person to become unattractive. A slovenly wife makes a truant husband.

Well, Julia thought, Rule 1 shouldn't pose much of a problem. Her tastes were sophisticated, but so too were Bill's. Surely, the purchase of a few nice things wouldn't threaten his masculinity?

Likewise, for Rule 2. She was all for keeping a clean house. But did Bill really expect her to be dusting and vacuuming? Surely a man with his resources would spring for a maid?

Regarding Rule 3, Julia understood the importance of appearances. Hers would be maintained, regardless of their future together.

Rule 4 read: "Do not receive attention from other men. Husbands are often jealous and some are suspicious without cause. Do not supply the cause!"

Actually, thought Julia, that wasn't bad advice. Bill was possessive and made no secret of it. She knew all about the phone calls he'd made before popping the question. Pointed calls to specific men with whom she had a history. If she said "yes," Rule 4 might be worth heeding.

Rule 5 was "Do not resent reasonable discipline of children by their father. Mothers should not assume that all chastisement of a child by his father is severe and unjustifiable."

Not an issue, thought Julia. Bill already had five kids (six, if you believed the rumors). If he wanted to slap them around, that was none of her business.

Rule 6: "Do not spend too much time with your mother. You may easily, in such a way, spend too little time at home."

No worries there. If she said "yes," Bill would become her priority—a simple fact she and her mother would have to accept.

Rule 7: "Do not accept advice from neighbors. Have a plan of your own for the solution of home problems."

Neighbors? thought Julia. What neighbors? Julia doubted that there would be any neighbors at all. As for a plan of her own, that was a given. Julia never did anything without a plan.

Rule 8: "Do not disparage your husband."

Funny, thought Julia, Bill is basically in the disparagement business. And what nasty thing could she possibly say that hadn't been said a thousand times already?

Rule 9: "Smile. Be attentive in little things. An indifferent wife is often supplanted by an ardent mistress."

Julia snorted. Bill had a mistress and everyone knew it, as well as a wife. But Julia understood attention to detail. Indeed, it was her obsession with the little things that had attracted Bill in the first place.

Rule 10: "Be tactful. Men, in the last analysis, are but overgrown children. They do not mind coaxing, but they resent coercion. Femininity attracts and compels them. Masculinity in the female repels."

Julia snorted more loudly this time. She knew that certain men were impervious to feminine wiles, just as certain women were immune to the charms of men. It was a fact to which she could personally attest. Yet here she was, a single woman who'd been whisked away to this most romantic of locations to ponder a proposal from a married man with a mistress who'd promised to make all her dreams come true.

Bill emerged from his tent holding two cups of coffee. Julia folded the newspaper and tucked it under her arm. They stood together in silence, sipping their coffee, admiring the wildflowers, the beach, the Pacific.

"Location, location, location," said Bill.

"It is a good one," Julia agreed.

"Have you come to a decision?"

"I have."

She turned to face Bill, who owned the newspaper tucked under her arm. She considered his reputation, his penchant for "yellow" journalism, for printing wild rumors and spurious gossip. She also considered his budget.

"Are you sure you want me?" Julia asked. "I'm not your typical homemaker."

Bill grinned. "I don't want a typical homemaker," he said. "I want to build a home with you."

She took a deep breath and nodded. "Okay," she said. "Let's do it."

And so they did. Right there on a sloping hill covered with wildflowers.

As always, Julia began with a plan. When construction ended three decades later, Bill's family campground had been transformed into 123 acres of gardens, terraces, pools, and walkways—a zoo filled with exotic creatures—and in the center of it all, a new home with 165 separate rooms designed by the homemaker who'd had the good sense to accept Bill's proposal.

No, no, not a marriage proposal—a business proposal. A proposal to build a home unlike any other, made to the first female architect licensed by the state of California. A woman who left behind seven hundred unique buildings and homes, all marked by her tireless attention to detail and unwavering commitment to satisfy her many clients.

Say what you want about Bill. Back in 1919, when Americans believed a woman's place was in the home, he hired a homemaker to build one. A woman who shared her client's belief that a man's home was his castle. In this case, a castle by the sea, built by a trailblazing architect named Julia Morgan and made famous by the king who lived there.

A king of media named . . . William Randolph Hearst.

I lived in a castle, once upon a time. Not like Hearst Castle but not unlike it, either. I wound up there because I'd been renting a room from a man who turned out not to own the room in question. This was a complicated, awkward situation that left me with less than forty-eight hours to find a new place to live and filled me with a level of domestic anxiety that briefly eclipsed the uncertainty surrounding my budding career in home shopping.

The year was 1990. I'd been at QVC for three whole months. Now I was on the verge of sleeping in my car—a poor calling card for an aspiring TV personality with dreams of working in prime time. So I turned to the classifieds and found an ad in the real estate section that was impossible to ignore. "Owner of large country estate seeks discreet 'caretaker' to oversee home and grounds," it read. "Free rent. Utilities included."

It wasn't the "free rent" that caught my eye or even the "country estate." It was the quotation marks around "caretaker." I understood what a caretaker does. But a "caretaker"?

The secretary who took my call told me that her employer was seeking a "discreet gentleman" to occupy a mansion she owned on a three-hundred-acre estate in Pennsylvania horse country.

The mansion was called Georgia Farm.

"Really?" I said. "Your boss wants someone to live in her mansion rent free?"

"Someone discreet."

"How about someone confused?"

"I beg your pardon?"

"I'm not sure I understand. What exactly would I be doing there, aside from being discreet?"

"Very little," she said. "There's already a caretaker on the premises. He and his wife live in a separate building behind the barn. All that you have to do is occupy the main house and assist my employer . . . as directed."

"I see," I said. "Your employer is seeking . . . companionship?"

The secretary giggled. "Oh, no," she said. "My employer has all the company she requires. You'll live alone at Georgia Farm."

"Alone?"

"And *discreetly*."

It was an utterly baffling phone call. But the secretary was nice. She sounded sane and seemed to like me. There and then, she arranged a time for an interview with her employer.

"Time is of the essence," she said.

"Tell me about it," I said.

Marion Boulton Stroud was the socialite's name. Her friends called her "Kippy." I met her a few hours later on the patio of the Marshalton Inn, just outside Philadelphia. It was unusually warm for late October, but thanks to Joe, the bartender, my Heineken was unusually cold—just what I needed to process Kippy's story.

Kippy told me that Georgia Farm had been her childhood home. According to her, it was idyllic, exquisite—a perfect place—and now she had inherited it.

"Well, then," I said. "Why don't you just move in?"

"I'd like to," she said. "But my father's still there. We've never gotten along. Not even a little."

"Who did you inherit the estate from?"

"My father, Morris Stroud. He died last year."

"But your father . . . he's still in the house?"

"Oh, yes. He walks the grounds at night. In the evenings, he sits in the great room by the fire."

Kippy was in her mid-fifties, well put together, and matter-of-fact. Like her secretary, she seemed sane.

"And you want a caretaker who isn't a caretaker because . . . ?"

Kippy smiled patiently and addressed me as she would a child. "The terms of my father's will are problematic. Georgia Farm is mine for as long as I want to live there. I inherited that right without inheriting the actual property. But if I don't move in within a year of his death, the estate goes to the Natural Lands trust. They're itching to get their hands on it."

"And you don't want that to happen?"

"No. Not yet, anyway."

"But you're scared to move in because your father is still walking the grounds."

"Yes. Something like that."

"And what is it you'd need me to do?"

"If people from the trust come poking around, as they surely will, you will tell them I live there. When they ask you where I am, you will tell them I'm traveling. When they ask who you are, you will tell them that you are my lover."

I nodded to Joe, who brought me another Heineken.

"Just to be clear, we're not going to be lovers. Are we?"

"Of course not," said Kippy. "But feel free to invite them into the house. Show them where we sleep. The closet's filled with my old clothes."

"And your father? What should I tell him if he starts to ask questions?"

"Handle the ghost of my father as you see fit," she told me. "My hope is that he will eventually move on, so that I can move in. Until he does, I won't return to Georgia Farm. But in the meantime, I don't wish to lose my right to live there."

"Even though you don't want to?"

"Precisely," she said. "Even though I don't want to."

It was the strangest offer I'd ever received, but given the circumstances, it was an offer I couldn't refuse. And so, on Halloween, I moved into the mansion and started in on the strangest year of my life thus far. Strange, because Kippy turned out to be right.

Georgia Farm really was haunted. . . .

THE BISCUIT BOMB

Rodman looked constipated. The young private's expression was one of perpetual concentration, punctuated from time to time by a crooked smile that sometimes appeared, apropos of nothing.

His best friend, on the other hand? Private Levy was the undisputed life of the platoon. In the barracks and on the battlefield, too, he'd proven to be a consummate storyteller. In a matter of minutes, Private Levy's stories could transport his fellow soldiers out of whatever fresh hell they'd found themselves in. Indeed, his love of a good story would impact not only the lives of his fellow soldiers—it would transform the careers of Dennis Hopper, Robert Redford, Robert Duvall, Lee Marvin, William Shatner, Peter Falk, Elizabeth Montgomery, Jack Klugman, Carol Burnett . . . the list goes on. In fact, you could argue that *The Sopranos*, *Breaking Bad*, and many other classic TV shows would never have come to be if not for the extraordinary contribution this nineteen-year-old private made during the Second World War.

But of the many stories that Private Levy would tell, the one that had the most impact unfolded beneath a palm tree on the bloody beach of a tiny island that most Americans couldn't have found on a map.

Rodman was there on that day—December 18, 1944—along with the rest of the platoon, and they were all hanging on Melvin Levy's every word. The boys of the 511th Parachute Infantry Regiment had spent a week fighting their way through the jungle, crawling through mud, slithering under barbed wire, and dying in record numbers. They'd lost 50 percent of their original complement—yet, in the midst of the madness and mayhem, there stood Private Levy, holding court under a palm tree in tropical heat, weaving his spell and getting laughs in a country where laughter was no longer among the indigenous sounds.

Rodman stood off to the side, smiling his crooked smile, looking vaguely constipated, and marveling at his friend's way with a story.

At that very moment, high over their heads and maybe a quarter mile to the south, a bombardier opened the doors of his DC-3. The payload left the plane cleanly and began to accelerate with the velocity one might associate with a 4,200-pound crate of K rations, dry sausages, chocolate bars, and hard biscuits. The boys called those crates "biscuit bombs," and with no supply lines to rely upon, they waited with great anticipation for those lifesavers to float down from the skies.

Down at ground level, the men of the 511th were spellbound. Private Levy was working up to the climax of his tale. All of his stories had surprising twists, and the men had no idea where this one was headed. For a few brief moments, the exhausted soldiers forgot all about the enemy that surrounded them, as well as their gnawing hunger. They had all lost themselves in Private Levy's unpredictable narrative.

Meanwhile, four hundred feet above the beach, the parachute of one of the biscuit bombs failed to deploy. One hundred feet after that, two tons of airborne grub reached terminal velocity.

Private Levy had just arrived at his surprising, hysterical punch line. The men had dissolved in fits of laughter and broken into applause. Private Levy took a few steps toward Rodman to bum a cigarette.

Rodman handed him one he'd just lit and fished another out of his fatigues.

Twenty feet over their heads, the biscuit bomb was moving at roughly 200 miles per hour. A split second later, it landed directly on Private Levy, and . . . that was that. The soldier was pulverized by the care package that had been meant to save his life.

That man, Private Levy, transformed television—but not by forming a legendary studio, starting a talent agency, or pioneering a technical breakthrough. No. All he did was die a few feet in front of his best friend in the most ironic manner you could imagine.

That evening, Rodman—the only other Jewish kid in the platoon—wrote a eulogy for Private Levy. The next morning, he read that eulogy to the rest of the platoon in a crisp, well-modulated baritone. His words, carefully measured and delivered with great deliberation, articulated the underlying dread of living in a world beyond his understanding—a world where certainty was not for sale. A world where a giant box of biscuits could plummet out of the heavens and pulverize your best friend.

War changes people, and Rodman was forever changed by the unlikely demise of Private Melvin Levy. He retained his crooked smile, his stilted delivery, and his vague look of chronic constipation. But from that moment on, the die was cast. Private Levy's surreal, gruesome passing had opened a door through which Rodman willingly walked.

A door . . . to another dimension. A dimension not only of sight and sound, but of mind. For that was the moment that a young private named Rodman Edward Serling first entered . . . the Twilight Zone.

You want to hear a ghost story?

I don't blame you. As the narrator of cultural touchstones like *Ghost Lab* and *Ghost Hunters*, I'm partial to them myself. But the only ghost story I know to be true is the one I experienced firsthand at Georgia Farm.

On my very first night in the mansion I sat alone by a fire in the Great Room, where the severed heads of various animals loomed all around me. I was reading a mystery when, all of a sudden, the player piano sprang into action. The tune was "Georgy Girl"—a burst of sound that sent me rocketing out of the chair like a marionette yanked upward by some spastic puppeteer. I don't remember dropping my scotch on my way out the door. I just remember cleaning it up later, along with the shattered glass, while the player piano continued to roll on its own.

That first night set the tone for the year that followed. Life at Georgia Farm was shot through with a strange feeling that shadowed my every move in the enormous home, which was not my own home: a fully furnished mansion, with back stairways that led to hidden rooms and grand fireplaces big enough to stand in. A home built in 1740 and filled with the possessions of the last man who'd died there: a smoking jacket (velvet); a humidor (fully stocked); a gun rack with shotguns and rifles (antique); a liquor cabinet (also fully stocked); as well as that player piano with a mind of its own.

That strange feeling was magnified by the strangeness of my new job. The graveyard shift at QVC had turned my days and nights upside down, leaving me in a permanent state of semiconsciousness. I'd leave for work at one in the morning, pausing on the way out to consider my reflection in an enormous mirror that hung in the vestibule. Suit and tie. Freshly shaven. Did I look like a man who'd been singing opera for a living one month earlier? Did I look like a man about to discuss the timeless appeal of collectible dolls and fake diamonds? I didn't know, but I was starting to see my late-night interactions with narcoleptic shopaholics in a whole new light. There were so many people out there eager to connect with a kindred spirit—even if that connection was going to cost them just three easy payments of $19.99.

Georgia Farm was just eight miles away from QVC's studio in West Chester, but the first few miles were country lanes. That made coming home from work a journey away from civilization. The driveway that led up to the main house was a mile long, at least; a gravel road that took its time winding up and around the old barn, went over a series of cattle guards, and ended at the top of the hill, where the house sat. It had an enormous porch with white pillars, a wide, sloping lawn that led down to a stone retaining wall, and beyond that, a lake stocked with perch and trout. Most mornings, I'd come home from work and sit on the porch, sipping a dead man's scotch. I'd watch the sunrise and go over the most meaningful interactions I'd had that day—conversations with disembodied voices who'd called in to talk to me while I was on air.

It was a lonely time, unsettled and unsettling. Sometimes, on the weekends, I'd have coworkers over. I encouraged them to bring friends, and word must have gotten around: one Saturday in early September, two hundred people came by for an impromptu lawn party. Joe, the bartender, brought bushels of oysters and a couple of kegs, which he tapped on the veranda. I must have been an odd sight, dressed as I was in Mr. Stroud's smoking jacket, sitting on the porch with an antique shotgun across my lap. No one seemed to know who I was and, as a man hired for his discretion, I couldn't really answer their questions. I let my guests assume what they wanted, knowing that whoever they thought I might be wasn't me. Sometime after midnight, the player piano started in on an old song I'd learned from Fred King:

People who pass me in pairs,
Act like the sidewalks are theirs
Old friends seem to be total strangers to me
For I'm so alone in the crowd.

That's how I felt at the end of that party: alone in the crowd. Then winter came to Georgia Farm, and I was alone for real.

Before long, a blizzard dumped two feet of snow over Pennsylvania horse country. I was unable to get to the studio or anywhere else for the better part of a week. I lost phone service, but a generator in the barn kept the power on—for which I was most grateful. Without electricity, I would have lost my mind. Although if you saw the videos I made during that period, you might assume I had lost it already.

One evening, I set a camcorder on a tripod, trained the lens on the player piano, and hit "record." The fireplace crackled in the background as I entered the frame, walking confidently, dressed in one of Mr. Stroud's many tuxedos, which fit surprisingly well. Nodding to my imaginary audience, I took a seat behind the ivories and flipped a switch under the keyboard. The tune was "Mr. Bojangles," and as the keys began to move, up and down, on their own, I pretended to push them—pantomiming with all the verisimilitude I could muster. When the roll ended, I rose, bowed, and exited the frame. That night, I watched the footage, and evaluated my performance. Did this handsome pianist look at all like Glen Gould? Why yes, I thought. Yes, he did.

In the morning, I took a revolver down to the lake. Carefully, I set the camera in the crook of a tree, pointed it over the frozen surface, and hit "record." The woods in the distance were dark and deep, but on this day I had no promises to keep. Only time to kill.

That night, I watched the footage and evaluated my performance. Who was this dangerous drifter, dressed in a cowboy hat and serape? This ominous hombre who wheeled around, drew his revolver with lightning speed, and took six imaginary enemies down in the blink of an eye? Did this gunslinger resemble Clint Eastwood? Why yes, I thought. Yes, he did. With a few more days of stubble, there'd be no difference at all.

The months went by. Spring came and then summer and fall. I never did see the ghost of Morris Stroud. The player piano turned out not to have a mind of its own—only a timer that sometimes malfunctioned. Creaks and rattles I'd hear in the night all turned out to be just creaks and rattles. But again, Georgia Farm was haunted—haunted by the man who stood in the vestibule every morning at 1:00 a.m., staring into that enormous mirror, thinking about who he was and what was happening to him. A friendly ghost, to be sure, but a ghost all the same. A kindly spirit who still looked a little like me.

THE MEN BEHIND BARS

Jimmy ran a very successful business for a very large company in a very competitive industry. After just two years, his revenues were in the tens of millions of dollars—and his customers were hopelessly addicted. The boss was pleased. Very pleased. But on February 12, 1985, Nicky turned up dead, and things got complicated.

Nicky was not the biggest earner on Jimmy's crew, but he was, in many ways, the most important. Nicky wasn't just an earner; he was the heart and soul of Jimmy's operation, and his death left a big hole—a hole that had to be filled immediately. But who could fill it? Jimmy set out to find a replacement for that which had been irreplaceable.

At the same time, halfway across the country, an Indiana farm boy wrestled with a very different kind of challenge. Tracy's dad had been arrested for murder and sentenced to life in prison. Clearly, the conviction was a bum rap. The state had spent millions of dollars prosecuting Tracy's dad, while the defense had spent less than $7,000 defending him. Plus, the wise guy who'd allegedly hired the boy's dad to murder a judge had been released in some kind of plea bargain. To top it all off, the judge who had condemned Tracy's father to a life behind bars had been one of the victim's pallbearers!

The whole setup stunk. Tracy was determined to get his dad an appeal. Of course, that would require the services of a *real* lawyer—something that would cost real money. So the twenty-four-year-old farm boy from Indiana did what he felt he had to do: he assumed a new identity and went looking for the kind of job that paid the kind of money he needed.

Tracy had no experience in this line of work, but he knew a few people who could possibly arrange a few introductions—and one of those people knew a guy, who introduced him to another guy, who arranged for a meeting with Jimmy.

It was a pivotal moment for the kid from Indiana. There was no denying his nervousness when he walked into Jimmy's bar for a sit-down.

"You know who I am?"

Tracy nodded. "Yes, sir. You're Jimmy, though I'm not sure if that's what I should call you. Sir."

Jimmy smiled. The kid had an openness about him. An undeniable midwestern likability that could be . . . useful—assuming he possessed other, necessary qualities that could make up for the loss of Nicky's unique set of talents.

Jimmy and Tracy talked at length. Then Jimmy introduced him to his crew. It was important that everyone be comfortable with Nicky's potential replacement—essential, in fact. Jimmy even asked Tracy to have a brief conversation with a few of his best customers, including a psychiatrist, to get a better sense of how he might cope with the pressures and challenges of Jimmy's operation.

It was a leap of faith, sure. But decisions like that often are. So, Jimmy hired the kid from Indiana to fill Nicky's shoes—and to everyone's relief, Tracy fit right in. Not only did the work come naturally, the money was even better than he'd imagined. A *lot* better. Before long, he had enough to hire the best attorneys in the country and set them to work, reviewing the dubious case that had landed his dad in a maximum-security prison.

Tracy would spend many years and many millions of dollars trying to get his father a second chance. But it was all for naught. Even the brilliant Alan Dershowitz, with his Harvard Law School professorship and the team of legal eagles that he had assembled, failed to get an appeal through the courts. Maybe it was because it wasn't the first time that Tracy's father had been charged with murder.

Nor was it the second time.

The truth is, Tracy's dad really *was* a hit man—a natural-born killer. And even though the circumstances surrounding his final conviction were undeniably squishy, the totality of his life was not exactly consistent with that of a model citizen. That was why he was denied his appeal. That's why he died behind bars, twenty-two years after his son walked into one to interview for the job that changed his career.

It's worth noting, though, that although Tracy worked at Jimmy's bar every day, he kept his dad's personal drama to himself. He knew that Jimmy's customers didn't want to hear a sad story about some kid from Indiana whose dad had turned out to be a murderer. They just wanted to relax in a friendly place where they all knew one another. Tracy also knew that Jim Burrows had given him more than a chance to pour beer in America's favorite bar—he had given him a chance to become America's favorite bartender, just as his predecessor, Nicky, had been. Nicky Colasanto, the actor who'd given us a lovable character named "Coach."

That's how Charles Voyde Harrelson wound up behind bars, in a cold and lonely place where everybody knew his name. And that's how his son, Woodrow Tracy Harrelson, became Woody Boyd: a man who spent eight years in a much friendlier joint, working behind the bar in a place called . . . Cheers.

"To live outside the law, you must be honest."

That's a direct quote from Bob Dylan, and it came to mind while I was sitting at the bar in Grumpy's, writing the story you've just read. Was Charles Harrelson an honest man? Was he honest with his fellow criminals? Was he honest with his son? With himself?

The bartender at Grumpy's had no answers, but wanted me to know that Bob Dylan was his favorite artist of all time. "An absolute genius," he said. "Why don't you write a story about him? Did you know he won a Nobel Prize?"

I swallowed some Anchor Steam and nodded. "I heard about that," I said. "Maybe I will."

I never did write that story. But if I had, I'd have called it "The Big Lie"—because Bob Dylan was not what you'd call a slave to the truth.

It's true. Bob Dylan lied his way through countless press conferences. He swiped melodies, arrangements, and lyrics from friends and forebears alike. His own memoir contains multiple lines lifted from various sources, and his Nobel Prize lecture, in 2017, contained twenty passages pilfered from the SparkNotes summary of *Moby-Dick*. Even the quote I've just attributed to him is another way of saying "honor among thieves." That concept was first discussed in Plato's *Republic*, then by Shakespeare in *Henry IV*, and then in every movie ever made about the mob and the importance of not being a rat. Which begs a bigger question: Why the hell would anyone ever believe anything Bob Dylan says? And that question reminds me of my good friend Jon Stewart.

Long before fake news became a real problem for genuine journalists, there was a real show about genuine news with fake journalists: *The Daily Show*. On that show, Jon Stewart lampooned every single pretense of news production. The overly dramatic music, the movie-trailer voiceovers, the ridiculous graphics, the desperate attempts by achingly earnest anchormen to make us believe they weren't reading someone else's words off a teleprompter: that was all perfect fodder for satire.

But a funny thing happened to my friend Jon Stewart: The less earnest he appeared to be, the more trusted he became. And the more trusted he became, the more seriously he was taken. It was fascinating to watch, especially when people disagreed with him. "Hey, folks," he said. "What's the problem here? I'm just a guy telling jokes." But now that everyone trusted him, no one believed him. Poor Jon. He simply couldn't have it both ways. Suddenly, millions of people were turning to *The Daily Show* for actual news—Jon Stewart was "more trusted" than every actual anchorman out there—and Comedy Central was "more credible" than FOX and CNN. Is it any wonder fake news became a real thing?

Speaking of lies: Let's assume, for a moment, that no one on television tells the truth, ever. (Trust me on this one, it's not a stretch.) One day, I appear on your TV screen and say, "Hi, I'm Mike Rowe, and I'm lying to you!"

Would that statement be true? It couldn't be, right? Because by definition, everyone on TV lies, all the time. But if I confess that I'm lying, in a place where no one ever tells the truth, wouldn't that make my confession . . . fundamentally honest? If so, would it not therefore be more accurate to say that the only way to be completely authentic in a place where everybody lies is to never tell the truth?

The answer, my friend, is blowin' in the wind, but I take comfort in something my father used to say: "A promise made is a debt unpaid." When it comes to trustworthiness, that strikes me as a sensible statement. But down here at Grumpy's, where I like to go after explaining *How the Universe Works* to my trillions of viewers, my ethics tend to be a bit more situational. So I'm going to have one more Anchor Steam and think seriously about the pros and cons of plagiarizing the next chapter and dedicating it to my good friend Bob Dylan.

THE CHERRY PIE IS TO DIE FOR

(For Bob Dylan)

Ted stands perfectly still in the Louisiana woods and looks for signs of prey. He loves to hunt, but today he'd rather be home. The heat is stifling, the rifle feels heavy in his hands, and there's no sign of game. Ted allows his mind to wander, and before long, he's thinking about the waitress in Dallas . . . the one he met five years ago. The one who got away.

They'd met at the lunch counter at Marco's. He'd been a postal worker back then and had stopped in one afternoon for a quick bite. The waitress hadn't noticed him at first. She'd been writing something.

"Must be mighty important," Ted said, "to make such a pretty face scrunch up like that."

The waitress jumped at the sound of his voice. "Sorry, mister. I was someplace else. What can I get you?"

She was a tiny thing, not even five feet tall. Her blond hair was uncombed, and her eyes were wide and very blue.

"I'd like a BLT," said Ted. "And a cup of coffee."

"You got it, but save some room for dessert. The cherry pie is to die for."

"Thanks," said Ted. "I'll do that."

The waitress wrote up his order, passed it to the cook, and went back to her papers.

"What are you working on?" Ted asked.

"Oh, nothing," she said. "Just a poem."

"What's it about?"

The waitress considered the postal worker. He had a warm smile—and a trustworthy face.

"It's about a nice boy who falls in love with the wrong girl."

"Maybe you'd like to read it to me?" said Ted, and that's what the waitress did:

You don't want to marry me honey,
Though just to hear you ask me is sweet;
If you did you'd regret it tomorrow
For I'm only a girl of the street.
Time was when I'd gladly have listened,
Before I was tainted with shame,
But it wouldn't be fair to you honey;
Men laugh when they mention my name.

Back there on the farm in Nebraska,
I might have said yes to you then,
When I thought the world was a playground,
Just teeming with Santa Claus men.
But I left the old home for the city,
To play in its mad, dirty whirl,
Never knowing how little of pity,
It holds for a slip of a girl.

The waitress stopped reading. "That's all I got," she said. "What do you think?"

"Well," said Ted, "I'm hoping for a happy ending."

The waitress offered a sad little smile. "Aren't we all, mister . . . aren't we all."

Five years have gone by, and Ted hears a sound that yanks him back to the hunt. Something is approaching in the distance. Something large. Ted clicks off the safety of his rifle and waits to see what might appear in the clearing. He understands the stakes. He understands the danger. But his thoughts are still on the waitress. He recalls their second meeting. She was still behind the counter at Marco's when he walked into the joint. Still writing. Still lovely. Her pretty face still scrunched up in concentration.

"You were right," said Ted. "The cherry pie was to die for."

Once again the waitress jumped at the sound of his voice. "You gotta quit sneaking up on me, mister!"

Ted laughed. "Sorry about that. I thought you saw me come in."

The waitress poured him some coffee.

"How's the poem coming?" he asked.

"Chipping away at it."

She picked up where she'd left off, reading quietly so that the other customers couldn't hear. Her lips were very close to Ted's ear:

I soon got a job in the chorus,
With nothing but looks and a form,
I had a new man every evening,
My kisses were thrilling and warm.

Then I fell for the "line" of a "junker,"
A slim devotee of hop,
And those dreams in the juice of a poppy
Had got me before I could stop.
But I didn't care while he loved me,
Just to lie in his arms was delight,
But his ardor grew cold and he left me;
In a Chinatown "hop-joint" one night.

The waitress paused and brushed away a tear. Ted wanted to take her hand. He wanted to comfort her. He wanted to tell her that people can change. Even a girl from the street. But the waitress wasn't quite finished.

Don't spring that old gag of reforming,
A girl hardly ever goes back,
Too many are eager and waiting;
To guide her feet off of the track.
A man can break every commandment
And the world will still lend him a hand,
Yet a girl that has loved, but un-wisely
Is an outcast all over the land.

Ted could take no more. He'd never seen so much sadness in such a pretty face.

"Listen to me," he said. "One day, a man is going to walk through those doors and sweep you off your feet. A good man. A man who doesn't care about your past. And from that moment on, your life will never be the same."

"Do you really think so?"

Ted looked earnestly into her wide blue eyes and said, "Maybe he already has."

For the next three months, the postal worker stopped by every day for a quick bite with some poetry on the side—and for a while there, it looked like the waitress might write him into her story. But one day, she was gone. Her replacement, Edna, was a sixty-five-year-old grandmother with a snaggletooth. It was Edna who gave poor Ted the bad news.

"Dunno where she went," said Edna. "Said she wouldn't be back. Said she found the love of her life. Now, what can I get ya?"

Ted was stunned. He swallowed hard and looked blankly down at the menu. But the menu had nothing he wanted.

Edna poured him some coffee. "Try the cherry pie," she said. "It's to die for."

Even now, five years later, hidden in the Louisiana woods, Ted can remember the heartbreak he felt that day. Even as his prey draws ever closer. Even as his fellow hunters raise their rifles alongside his. Even as the stolen Ford crests the hill on Highway 154 and slows down at the intersection in the clearing. Even as he and the rest of the posse open fire with tommy guns from the woods on the side of the road.

When the shooting finally stops, 136 rounds of hot lead have perforated the stolen Ford. Many of those bullets have also perforated the man behind the wheel. Then the smoke clears and Ted slowly approaches what's left of the driver. It's him, all right. Justice has finally caught up with the bank robber who's killed twelve cops in cold blood. Now Ted considers the passenger. She's a tiny thing, a slip of a girl, not even five feet tall. Her blond hair is uncombed. Her dead eyes are wide open and very blue. He hangs his head, closes his own eyes, and recalls the final stanza from the poem she'd read him five years ago:

> *You see how it is don't you honey,*
> *I'd marry you now if I could,*
> *I'd go with you back to the country,*
> *But I know it won't do any good,*
> *For I'm only a poor branded woman*
> *And I can't get away from the past.*
> *Good-bye and God bless you for asking*
> *But I'll stick it out now till the last.*

You might not have heard of Ted Hinton, the postal worker turned deputy sheriff who was hired to hunt down the notorious bank robber. You might not remember a poem called "The Street Girl." But you've probably heard of the waitress who wrote it: the woman who got away, until she didn't. An aspiring poet, whose only appearance in print was in the headlines and on Most Wanted posters. A famous outlaw named . . . Bonnie Parker.

What if Bonnie had taken a flyer on Ted? She didn't know him from Adam, and yet there was something between them. Ted had felt it. Had Bonnie felt it too? He might have kept on working for the post office. She might have kept on being a waitress, or become a published poet. Together, they might have been happy—as I was, when a woman named Joan took a flyer on me.

It was September 1991. I had been fired from QVC a few months earlier (justifiably), rehired (inexplicably), then banished—sent back to the graveyard shift for my sins (permanently). Then a nasty flu had gone around, and most of the prime-time hosts had gone home, where they'd been now for several days, puking their guts up. I'd been called in to fill in for the stricken, and I was halfway through a riveting hour called *Ideas to Make Your Life Easier* when Joan walked into the studio.

Rivers was the Joan in question. A mythical figure who'd come up the hard way in the business, enduring ups and downs that would have crushed lesser women. She was a genius, a legend, a rebel. She was the Bonnie Parker of comedy. I had never met her, but I knew who she was, and it was unthinkable to me that my bosses would turn her loose on QVC's G-rated audience. Stranger still, that they would allow her to share the same stage with me. And yet, there she was.

Rivers was there to promote her line of clothing and jewelry. She had been scheduled to appear that morning with a real, reputable host. But on her way to the greenroom, she had stopped to watch as I sang a tune from *Mack and Mabel*, hoping to boost the sales of a portable karaoke machine. When I was done, she pulled something out of her giant purse, walked onto the set, and began asking questions—right there, on live television.

"Oh, my God. Where did you get that *tie*?"

"I beg your pardon?"

"Your tie," she said. "It's awful. Did you steal it from a Lutheran?"

"I made it myself," I said. "On a loom in my attic."

"It's hideous, truly. And that suit? You look like an unmade bed."

"Thanks," I said. "It helps me sleep on the job. You look radiant, though, if I may be so bold."

"Look a little closer. One more face-lift, and I'll have a goatee."

It took me a second, but the image sunk in. I may have chortled. I may have even guffawed. If I had been wearing dentures, I might have spat them across the room.

"You seem like a nice young man. It's a shame you don't have any taste. Is there a woman in your life?"

"Several," I replied. "But none that compete with your years of experience."

Joan laughed. She gave me the finger. Then she presented me with a "Tie-Button Tie"—a fancy piece of silk with a buttonhole in the back that allowed a gentleman to affix the tie to the button on his shirt in a way that, in her words, was "simply to die for."

"It won't swing into your spaghetti sauce the next time you take one of your 'special ladies' out for a big night at the Olive Garden," she said.

Rivers told me all about the various trinkets and garments she'd come on to sell, including a simulated diamond set in 14-karat gold that, she suggested, would be perfect for any of the women in my life. ("Remember, ladies, fake jewelry doesn't have to make you look like a slut, even if you are one.") She described one stretch jersey as "a pretty little thing with a nice comfortable lining that won't get stuck in your ass crack." She made me laugh, both because she was funny and because I imagined my bosses recoiling in horror.

Joan wasn't off script—she was unscriptable. To me, that made her heroic.

I didn't see her again for a year and a half. By then, she had become a fixture at QVC, well on her way to selling a billion dollars' worth of stuff. Really: a billion. I, on the other hand, was still working the graveyard shift, still hawking products that appeared to have been sourced from the midway of some condemned carnival. Then I caught a break. QVC and CBS agreed to coproduce a pilot around Joan, tentatively called *Can We Shop?* Under the terms of the deal, Joan could select any QVC host to be her second banana, and she chose me.

I can't express how profoundly surprising that decision was— to me, to my fellow QVC hosts, and most of all to those who had consigned me to the graveyard shift. But Rivers insisted. The next thing I knew, I was sitting next to her on a soundstage in New York City, doing my very best Ed McMahon impression. Go figure.

In television, as in real life, you don't always know the significance of a thing when it happens. This was different. I knew exactly what it meant. Appearing on CBS with Joan Rivers was the first thing I'd done that looked halfway legitimate.

I left QVC soon after that—of my own volition. I never saw Rivers again. Not in person, anyway. Like the rest of the world, I saw her on the red carpet and watched her shenanigans here and there. How could I not? Icons have a way of being everywhere at once. I watched *A Piece of Work*, the fine documentary about her—I wanted to call her afterward and tell her how brave she'd been to be that forthcoming. I still wish I had. But I'll settle for my memories of a holiday party at her Fifth Avenue penthouse. It was a black-tie affair, but I wore one of her Tie-Button Ties. It amused her to no end. I brought her some cookies, too. Mom, upon learning that I would be visiting the actual home of a bona fide celebrity, was afraid I would arrive empty-handed or (worse) with a six-pack of Rolling Rock under my arm. She'd made a tin of chocolate chip cookies and told me to give them to "Mrs. Rivers," with her compliments. Which I did.

I don't know if Joan actually ate them, but she accepted them with grace and put them on the mantel next to her menorah.

A MANLY MAN,
A GOLD MEDAL,
AND A REALLY BIG SEA

Long before he won the gold medal that ended up on his mantel, the Manly Man stood in the sand at the tip of Balboa Peninsula, smoking a cigarette, staring at the biggest waves he'd ever seen.

"God Almighty," he said. "That is a *really* big sea."

The Olympic champion standing next to him smiled and nodded. Monstrous breakers, blown to towering heights by an offshore breeze, were being forced together at the last moment by a series of jetties that guarded Newport Harbor. Local surfers called it "the Wedge." Sensible people called it a death trap.

Wally O'Connor called it a challenge.

"You're right," said Wally. "This is a *very* big sea. Isn't it fantastic?"

The Manly Man felt the adrenaline course through his body. This was the way he felt every week on the gridiron, moments before the bone-jarring impact at the line of scrimmage would determine who remained standing and who got knocked to the ground. He was addicted to the feeling—which is why he was drawn to this dangerous new fad that Wally had come up with.

"I'll take the first pass," said Wally. "Watch and learn."

The Manly Man stepped back into the crowd, lit another Camel, and watched Wally O'Connor glide through the water. It was easy to see why he'd won gold in Paris. He ducked under one wave and then another, swimming hard against the riptide with long, powerful strokes. A hundred yards out, the water was only four feet deep, but the waves were at least eight feet in height—treacherous, to say the least. Wally waited for the wave he wanted, dove into its base, pushed hard off the shallow bottom, and burst out of the crest. Then he began to fly. At least that's how it looked to everyone who was watching.

Partially embedded in the curl of the surge, Wally eased himself into the pipeline while extending one hand in a "stop" gesture. His upturned palm carved into the great rumbling wall of water while his other arm remained tucked behind him. With white foam shooting off his chest and green water breaking over his head, Wally flew toward the shore like Superman. No one had ever seen anything like it—surfing without a board! As the mighty wave began to crash in around him, Wally stroked hard, staying just in front of the thunderous crash that sent him flying toward the beach like a human missile in a sea of foam, skimming across the surface before sliding gracefully onto the sand, where the locals greeted him with wild applause.

Wally stood, took a modest bow, and turned to the Manly Man who had yet to win a gold medal.

"You're up, champion. Ready?"

The big man nodded. "I am." A simple answer to a simple question that wound up changing the course of his life.

The Manly Man confronted the big sea with manly confidence, imitating everything he'd seen Wally do. He swam hard against the riptide for a hundred yards. He waited for a wave as big as Wally's had been. When it came, he dove into its base, pushed off the shallow bottom, and burst out of the white water—at which point he began to fly, just like Wally.

But here's the thing: if you're going to go toe-to-toe with the big sea, you'll need more than manly confidence; you'll need perfect timing. And when the wall of water began to fall apart all around him, the Manly Man was out of position. Thus his manly body was propelled with great velocity not toward the beach but rather, straight toward the shallow bottom.

Over the crashing roar of the surf—over the muted sound of his own screams—he heard the sounds of his future vanishing before him. The snap of his collarbone, the crack of his arm, the crunch of his shoulder as it popped out of its socket. Those were the sounds of a football scholarship coming to an end, along with his college education at USC and the law degree he had hoped to graduate with. All of it gone. Taken away by the really big sea.

In the back of the ambulance, broken and lucky to still be alive, the Manly Man lit another Camel. Did he foresee that the only job he'd be able to find in the course of that year would be in the props department at 20th Century Fox? Did he foresee that schlepping those props back and forth between sets would lead to an audition, which would ultimately require him to change his name to something more . . . masculine? Probably not. But one thing is for sure: the Manly Man could have *never* imagined the press conference he would hold in his living room thirty-five years later. The one conducted just four days after his surgery.

There, in his Encino home, the Manly Man, now with his Manly Name—but still no gold medal—gave an Oscar-worthy performance. Smiling bravely through unspeakable pain and talking with great confidence to the Hollywood press, he assured the reporters who'd gathered that he was ready to get back into the saddle. He didn't show them the giant purple scar around his left side. He didn't discuss the lung that had just been removed or the four ribs that he was now missing. He didn't mention the sutures that kept breaking open every time he coughed or the bucket of phlegm and sputum upstairs by his bed. As for the disease itself, he didn't even mention it by name.

"I've licked 'the Big C' before," he told the reporters. "And I'll lick it again. Trust me, fellas, when I go out, it'll be on both feet."

The reporters were delighted. No one had called it "the Big C" before. No one had ever dismissed it as nothing more than a mere nuisance. Surely, if anyone *could* beat the disease, it would be the Manly Man who'd reduced it to a nickname. And sure enough, he did, completing two dozen feature films over the course of the next twelve years—including the one that finally won him an Oscar.

But here's the thing—if you're gonna go toe-to-toe with the *really* Big C, you'll need more than manly confidence. *You'll need to stop smoking.* Unfortunately for the Manly Man, that was simply too much to ask. And so the man who had beaten the Japanese, the Mexicans, the Nazis, the Viet Cong, the Mongols, and too many Indians to count, in too many westerns to recall, was ultimately vanquished by a deadly horde of unfiltered Camels: five packs a day over the course of four decades and then some.

In the end, the man who'd shot Liberty Valance didn't possess the true grit to quit smoking.

Today, there's a cancer foundation that bears his Manly Name, along with a park in Newport Beach, an airport in Orange County, and the credits of more than two hundred films. It's the same name that's on the back of the gold medal he finally did get, in the hospital, one month before he died, in 1979: a Congressional Gold Medal embossed with the name that we all know today, thanks to the Manly Man's run-in with the really big sea—a run-in that changed his life—and the really Big C that ended it.

It was a shame but a pretty good run, all in all, for the kid who was born Marion Morrison and died a Manly Man named . . . John Wayne.

I was in Seattle filming the first round of *After the Catch*—a talk show that takes place in a bar. The setup was simple: captains and crew from *Deadliest Catch* gathered to chatter, confer, sometimes confabulate. I was the moderator. Picture a pre-hashtag *Charlie Rose* but with cigarettes and whiskey.

We were recording the show in real time (or something close to it), as though it were a live production. Producers, directors, and cameramen were milling about, positioning cameras around a big table, and setting up all kinds of lights. But I got the sense that nobody actually knew what was going to happen once shooting began—and that turned out to be the case. The captains sat down at the table; they didn't know what was happening, either. I wouldn't have called them nervous: these were manly men, too, after all. Let's call them "fidgety" and full of questions about how the day would unfold. I had no answers to give them. Unlike ship's captains, I prefer states of confusion—I think they make for good television—and I said as much. I also suggested that, given the setting, there were any number of remedies on hand that would take the edge off.

Only one of the captains seemed completely at ease: Phil Harris, who'd arrived at the last minute and done so in style, aboard a brand-new Harley-Davidson. He'd walked into the bar with a gargantuan smile on his face and said hello to each of the captains in turn before turning to me.

"Hey, Phil," I said. "How's it going?"

"I got nothing to say to you, Mike, until you ride my hog."

Resistance was futile. When Phil wanted something done, it got done—and his enthusiasm for whatever it was that had grabbed his attention was contagious. At sea, he focused on catching crab. At home, he focused on his boys, Josh and Jake. At the moment, he was focused on his new motorcycle—something that gave him so much joy he just had to share it with me. And he did. He insisted upon it. By the time I rode back into the parking lot, the other captains were in *very* good spirits.

Mind you, Phil wasn't perfect. He had a temper. He rode fast and drove fast. Like John Wayne, he smoked like a chimney, and—needless to say—he cursed like the sea dog he was. He'd been the captain of his boat, the *Cornelia Marie*, for close to two decades, and he liked to do things his way. But his way left a lot of room for other people. Once I ran into Phil in Las Vegas. I was speaking at the Conexpo Convention, and Phil happened to be there, manning a booth for a pulley company. During a break, I wandered over and watched him talk to his fans. There were many of them, *Deadliest Catch* fans who were delighted to see Phil in person. They wanted autographs, handshakes, a word or two with their favorite captain. The line grew and grew, but Phil had all the patience in the world for them. Standing behind a display, unobserved, I saw him focus completely on the person in front of him. He found something new and original to say every time. He answered questions that were way too personal and stayed well beyond his required time, waiting until the very last fan—an elderly gentleman—had gotten his turn. The gentleman called Phil "an American hero." Phil blushed, signed the man's hat, and talked to him for a long while.

Some people are better than others at this sort of thing. Phil was a natural. He handled the measure of fame that TV had brought him in the most genuine way: he acted as if he'd always had it. No matter who you were, you always got the same Phil.

Once, in LA, I attended some event the Discovery Channel had sponsored. Most of the captains were there, along with the Mythbusters, Bear Grylls . . . in short, all the usual suspects. Discovery Communications' CEO, David Zaslav, was there, too.

David Zaslav oversees the largest provider of nonfiction content in the world and does so with an attention span that rivals that of a fruit fly. It's true: he calls meetings that might be adjourned a minute or so after they've started. He's scary smart and not terribly patient with folks who don't keep up. He never sits still—he's *always* in motion and always surrounded by a human force field: a group of assistants whose primary task is to keep away those who might suck up his valuable time.

I watched him rush through the room; his retinue followed like the tail of a comet. He had already reached the back door when Phil walked in through the front, and what happened next is the honest truth.

David and Phil shook hands and started to chat.

Thirty seconds later, they were still talking.

A minute later . . . still talking.

People stopped what they were doing and started to stare, but five minutes later, David and Phil were still at it. Phil was doing most of the listening—David was talking intently—and we were all wondering: What could the crab boat captain and the media mogul possibly have in common? We watched in amazement as David and Phil wandered off to a corner, away from everyone else. There they sat down and continued to talk.

That was unprecedented. Every few minutes, an assistant slid over to give David an excuse to depart. Every time, David waved the assistant away. When Phil took out a cigarette and made as if he would light it indoors, David walked him outside. They stayed outside for more than an hour. Standing there. Talking. Just the two of them.

Eventually, after they'd said their good-byes, Phil joined me at the bar. "You know who that was?"

"Tell me," I said.

Phil threw back a poorly made duck fart. "That was the president of the whole damn channel."

"Actually," I said, "he's the CEO of the whole damn network."

"Is that right? Well, whatever. He seems like a nice guy. Kind of chatty, but his heart's in the right place."

For me, it comes down to this: we know a real thing when we see it and crave it because it's in such short supply. We seek it out, stand in line for a chance to be near it. Fans, fishermen, CEOs—they all saw Phil Harris for what he was. The real deal: flawed and human and decent and kind. When a monster wave sent him flying out of his bunk during a crucial run toward the end of the show's fourth season, Phil cracked a few ribs.

"I can't breathe," he kept saying (while smoking one cigarette after another).

There he was, toe-to-toe against the big Bering Sea. He was in terrible pain, but with 34,000 pounds left to catch, he dragged himself back to the cockpit, where he started coughing up blood—a fact that he kept from his sons and most of his men.

"Please don't say anything to my kids," he said to Todd Stanley—the cameraman who'd spent years filming Phil.

"Why?" Todd asked.

Pointing to the Bering Sea, Phil said, "Because I don't want them thinking about anything else than that. Or one of them will get hurt."

Phil ended up finishing his northern set, then made an hour run to his western strings, where he told Todd, "It's different when it's yourself and you're sitting here. Believe me, this isn't like a crew member getting hurt. I've got an obligation to the people I work for. To these guys, their families. The whole ball of wax is riding on my shoulders."

Twenty-four hours after that, he finally called in to a hospital. "I can't get in for a couple of days," he said.

By the time that he finally pulled into St. Paul with his men and their catch, he'd been in pain for sixty continuous hours. Down at the hospital, he was given a one-in-ten chance for survival. Along with the cracked ribs, he was diagnosed with a pulmonary embolism—a blood clot that had traveled up from his leg to his lungs. It should have killed him. I suppose you could argue it did, a few years later. The "Big C" didn't get him. Neither did the Big Sea. But those "little c's" he'd been puffing on since he was a kid hadn't done him any favors.

Anyway, back in 2008, Phil Harris recovered. He didn't quit smoking. Maybe he couldn't. But what he did do was continue to take care of his sons and his men. Steven Spielberg told David Zaslav, who told me, that the way Phil had acted after his injury was one of the bravest things Spielberg had seen. But the way I look at it is, Phil was just trying to get to the end of his story his way—and bringing his viewers along for the ride.

He really was one hell of a captain.

A TALE OF TWO PUPILS

George Underwood was fifteen years old when he punched his handsome saxophone player. His motivation? An unforgivable display of skulduggery that simply could not be ignored. A completely unacceptable betrayal made worse by the fact that the handsome saxophone player in question was George Underwood's best friend.

Here's what happened: In the spring of 1962, George and his best friend were pupils at the Bromley Technical High School for Boys. They played together in a band you've never heard of called George and the Dragons. The Dragons had real potential, though everyone agreed that George was the most likely member to find real fame. He had the looks for it, that's for sure. George was also handsome, remarkably so, and bursting with charisma. His personality leapt off the stage, he had a strong voice, and his Elvis impersonation never failed to make the young girls swoon.

Anyway, George had arranged for a date with Carol Goldsmith, the pretty schoolgirl he'd been eyeing all semester. But a few hours before they were supposed to meet down at the youth center, George's saxophone player pulled him aside.

"Hey, George, I just saw Carol down at the record store. She said to tell you she wouldn't be able to make it this evening. Between you and me, I think she's seeing someone else."

George was disappointed, obviously, but he appreciated the heads-up from his loyal bandmate. Future rock stars shouldn't be stood up in public by pretty schoolgirls. They had images to protect. But in reality, it was Carol Goldsmith who wound up waiting for George Underwood that night. She waited for over an hour and probably would have waited longer if the handsome saxophone player hadn't arrived in George's place.

"Hey, Carol! How's it going?"

"Oh," Carol said, "I was just waiting for George. He was supposed to be here an hour ago."

The saxophone player assumed a pensive expression and sighed deeply.

"Sorry, Carol. I saw George earlier today, and he told me he had other plans tonight. Between you and me, I think he's seeing someone else."

Carol Goldsmith was disappointed, obviously, but she appreciated hearing the truth. She also appreciated the saxophone player's sympathetic gaze.

"Thank you for telling me," said Carol. "By the way, you have pretty eyes."

The saxophone player smiled. "Thanks. Hey, you wanna go get some ice cream?"

The next day at school, George learned of this treachery and reacted as any young man filled with testosterone and righteous indignation would. He confronted his traitorous bandmate, confirmed his duplicity, and delivered a roundhouse: a mighty blow that left his best friend flat on his back with a black eye and a swollen face.

Actually, the fallout was worse than that. George Underwood's temper earned him the contempt of everyone at Bromley Tech, including that of his teachers, his best friend's parents, and Carol

Goldsmith. Sucker-punching the saxophone player led to the demise of George and the Dragons, as well. Why? Because with that one blow, George had forever changed his best friend's appearance—and in the process, the appearance of countless magazine covers: *Time*, *Esquire*, *GQ*, *People*, *Vanity Fair*, and, of course, *Rolling Stone*.

But all that would come later. On that particular day in 1962, George's saxophone player was rushed to the hospital, where he remained for several weeks as doctors tried to correct the damage George had inflicted. Fortunately, they did not succeed. The official diagnosis was "anisocoria," and after two surgeries, doctors said the damage was irreversible.

George would live with the guilt for the rest of his life. But he would not be unforgiven. In fact, a few months later, George and his saxophone player wound up in another band you've never heard of: the Konrads. After the Konrads, they formed the Hooker Brothers—which you've probably never heard of either—and then the King Bees, which also might not ring any bells.  Along the way, though, George came to realize that no matter what they called themselves, people were not coming to hear him sing; they were coming to see his deformed but still handsome saxophone player. The best friend whose face he had permanently altered.

The King Bees went their separate ways, too. Most bands do, and George Underwood shifted his focus to painting and drawing. Not as glamorous, perhaps, as being a rock star, but one plays the cards one gets—and, all things considered, George had some pretty good cards. Today you can see his artwork all over the world, and on the covers of more than a few albums. Albums from bands that you probably *have* heard of: T. Rex, Procol Harum, Mott the Hoople, and the Fixx. But, of course, his most famous album covers are the ones he did for his old friend—who, sadly, no longer plays the saxophone or anything else for that matter.

One evening—years before he died but long after he'd become a rock-and-roll legend—George Underwood's former saxophone player called and thanked him for that punch in the face. He could not have been more sincere. The anisocoria, he said, had given him an identity he never could have cultivated on his own. Thanks to that precipitous blow, landed back when they were both teenagers, his left pupil would remain permanently dilated. As a result, his eyes appeared to be two different colors—and *that* gave George Underwood's best friend a certain quality. A rock star quality. A quality that helped secure his appearance on countless magazine covers: *Time, Esquire, GQ, People, Vanity Fair*, and, of course, *Rolling Stone*.

On January 11, 2016, George Underwood learned that Ziggy would no longer play guitar. The Starman who gave us Major Tom and Life on Mars would never get to enjoy his Golden Years. George was heartbroken. And although Carol Goldsmith's feelings are not on the record, it's safe to assume that she, too, misses the Rebel Rebel who studied Fame and went on to define it. A pupil who stood out above all the others. A best friend named . . . David Bowie.

April 1984. A young Caucasian male was spotted behaving erratically on the streets of Baltimore. According to witnesses, he was wearing headphones and carrying a Walkman, but the sounds he was making were less than musical. They were the sounds of a crazy person having a loud conversation with himself. The witnesses were my parents. The Caucasian was me.

"You sound deranged."

"What?" I removed my headphones.

"Your father said you sound terrific," my mom said. "Better and better each time!"

"Do you even know what it is you're singing about?" my dad asked.

"Sort of," I said. "It's called 'The Coat Aria.' It's from *La Bohème*. It's a love song about a guy who gives his favorite coat to a girl who's dying of consumption."

"Tuberculosis, John. 'Consumption' is another word for tuberculosis."

"I know what consumption is, Peggy. I just don't know why Michael is singing Italian love songs about jackets."

Over dinner the night before, I'd told my father about a loophole that would have enabled me to start making some actual money in TV and radio. He hadn't understood that, either.

"I don't get it," he said. "You don't even like opera. You don't know anything about opera. Why are you auditioning for the opera?"

"Because the opera is under the jurisdiction of the American Guild of Musical Artists," I said. "If I can get into AGMA, then I become automatically eligible to join the Screen Actors Guild. If I can get into SAG, I can start making union commercials. And if I start making union commercials, I can start paying you rent."

"I like the sound of that. But if you want to be in SAG, why not just join SAG?"

"SAG won't let me join until I get work on a union job."

"Why don't you audition for union jobs?"

"Because the agents won't send me on union auditions unless I have my union card."

"That doesn't make any sense."

"No," I said. "It doesn't. But it does explain why people hate agents."

"It's a Catch-22, John. Do you remember that movie?"

"Yes, Peggy, I remember *Catch-22*. I read the book. It didn't make sense, either."

My father went back to his meat loaf. I put my headphones back on and listened to Samuel Ramey sing "The Coat Aria" for the fiftieth time. I didn't hear what my mother said next. It looked like "You're going to be terrific!"

The next morning, I drove downtown to an address on Charles Street where the Baltimore Opera Company rehearsed. My friend Mike Gellert was already waiting for me in his car.

"I've got the melody down," I told him. "The words are still a bit squishy."

"Hop in," he said. "Let's hear it."

Gellert had sung in the Baltimore Opera for years. He was also a fellow barbershopper. He'd told me about the opera loophole and encouraged me to audition in spite of my absolute lack of experience.

"They have open calls on the last Thursday of every month," he'd said. "What do you have to lose?"

I closed the passenger-side door and did my best impression of Samuel Ramey, the bass-baritone I'd been listening to for the last two days, singing the shortest aria I could find:

Vecchia zimarra, senti,
io resto al pian, tu ascendere
il sacro monte or devi.
Le mie grazie ricevi.
Mai non curvasti il logoro dorso
ai ricchi ed ai potenti.
Passâr nelle tue tasche
come in antri tranquilli
filosofi e poeti.

Ora che i giorni lieti fuggîr,
ti dico addio,
fedele amico mio,
addio, addio.

When I finished, Gellert said, "You're right. Your Italian really is terrible."

"Thanks," I said. "You should do motivational speeches."

"Don't worry about it," said Gellert. "They're desperate for young guys with low voices. You've got a shot. Just sing it like we rehearsed it, and don't sass the piano player."

We walked into the rehearsal hall and joined the half-dozen hopefuls waiting nervously in the lobby. At the far end of the hall, a soprano was singing the bejesus out of something so beautiful it made my eyes water: "O Mio Babbino Caro," from Puccini's *Gianni Schicchi*. When she finished, the man playing the piano said, "Thank you so much for your delightful audition. We have all the sopranos we need, but we'll keep your name on file and call if an opening presents itself. NEXT!"

"That's Bill Yannuzzi," said Gellert. "He's the musical director. He speaks five languages. He can play any aria from any opera from memory."

Next up, a tenor sang "Nessun Dorma," also by Puccini. He, too, sounded amazing and when he was finished, Mr. Yannuzzi said, "Thank you so much for your delightful audition. We have all the tenors we need, but we'll keep your name on file and call if an opening presents itself. NEXT!"

The next four hopefuls—two sopranos, one alto, and another tenor—all sounded like seasoned pros. They all got the same speech from the man at the keyboard. Thanks, but no, thanks. The next "NEXT!" was me.

Gellert handled the introduction. "Mr. Yannuzzi, this is my

friend Mike Rowe. He sings bass in a barbershop quartet. He can't read music, but he's got a low D and he's great onstage. I think he'd be an asset to the company. He's going to sing 'The Coat Aria' from *La Bohème*. Sort of."

Mr. Yannuzzi started to play. I started to sing but stopped a few measures in.

"Sorry," I said, "that's a lot higher than I rehearsed it. Can you play it in a different key?"

"I can play it in any key," said Mr. Yannuzzi. "What key do you prefer, if not the one Mr. Puccini intended?"

"I don't know," I said. "How about a manlier key?"

Mr. Yannuzzi looked at the chorus master, a man named Tom Hall. Mr. Hall shrugged and looked at Gellert, who sighed and said, "Play it in D."

Mr. Yannuzzi started again, a few steps lower than before. When I finished, he looked at me with an odd mix of curiosity and contempt. "Well, your Italian is terrible," he said, "and your phrasing is atrocious."

"Thanks," I said. "It's a gift."

"On the positive side," said Mr. Hall, "you sure do sing loud."

Both men looked more than a little skeptical as they weighed the pros and cons of letting an untrained barbershopper—a guy who couldn't read music—into their esteemed organization. Finally, Mr. Yannuzzi turned to Gellert.

"This man is your responsibility," he said. "Teach him Italian, Mr. Gellert. Teach him diction. Teach him intonation."

"Teach him to suck less," said Mr. Hall.

Gellert promised to do that very thing, and just like that I was in. The stage was set—for what, I wasn't entirely sure, but if I could fake my way into a reputable opera company, it was hard not to wonder what other stages might welcome the likes of me. . . .

OH, BROTHER!

Ed and his little brother had a lot in common. Both were famous actors. Both were deeply patriotic. They both loved turkey with all the fixings. But unfortunately for those around them, Ed was a staunch Republican, his brother was a devoted Democrat—and that was not a recipe for a peaceful Thanksgiving dinner.

Before the election the brothers had bickered over the economy, immigration, taxes, race relations, and, of course, the border. Their arguments had been heated but always respectful. It was frustrating for Ed, though, because during the runup to the recent election, his kid brother had been so damn smug. Like many in the entertainment business, Ed's little brother saw the election's outcome as a fait accompli. He not only believed that the Democrat would win—he believed it would happen in a landslide. All his friends said so. All the pundits said so. Besides, the Republican alternative was a buffoon. A dangerous, unpredictable buffoon.

Well, on November 8, conventional wisdom had gone out the window. The buffoon had won and now—after the most contentious election in US history—Ed's little brother was still in shock. He

wanted a recount. He wanted a do-over. Bits of mashed potato flew from his mouth as he announced to everyone in the room that the Republican was "not *my* president."

Ed held his tongue as his little brother railed against the electoral college, the new limits on a free press, the future of the Supreme Court, and, of course, the situation with the border. His face became flushed, and his voice rose higher and higher. It seemed to Ed that he was watching a performance—a series of talking points culled from a biased media, delivered with all the drama and passion he could muster, like a Shakespearean actor addressing the last row of a sold-out theater.

"The man is a tyrant," he said. "A warmonger. A dictator. And mark my words, he will destroy this country!"

With that, Ed's little brother stood up from the table, knocked his chair to the floor, and slammed the door so hard a picture fell off the wall. Ed sighed heavily and apologized to his guests. He turned his attention back to the turkey, and that . . . was that.

The two brothers never spoke again.

It's always a drag when politics trump family relations. But there was more to this sibling rivalry than a contentious election. While both brothers were actors, only one was a household name. It was Ed who traveled through Europe and toured the United States to great acclaim. It was Ed who basked in the glow of critical reviews after performing one hundred nights of *Hamlet* on Broadway. And it was Ed who would have his statue erected in Gramercy Park—the first American actor to be honored in such a way. Ed's fame cast a long shadow, and his little brother had lived in it for most of his life.

Yet we barely remember Ed today. His statue is still there, not far from Broadway, but his memorial is dwarfed by the legacy of his younger brother. Just five months after that fateful Thanksgiving dinner, the aspiring thespian stepped out from under his older brother's shadow and delivered *his* command performance. With just one line, delivered with all the drama and passion he could muster, Ed's little brother addressed the last row of a sold-out theater, just like the Shakespearean actor he had always wanted to be: "*Sic semper tyrannis!*"

"Thus always to tyrants."

It was an odd thing to say about a president whose most fervent hope had been to make America great again—by reuniting the North and the South and bringing an end to the civil war that had very nearly destroyed the country he'd served. But that's exactly what the audience at Ford's Theatre heard on that fateful night in April, just a few seconds after Edwin's little brother murdered Abraham Lincoln.

That's why we barely remember the immensely talented and deeply patriotic performer named Edwin Booth. The great actor upstaged by his younger brother—a common murderer, whose full name is unforgettable . . . and not worth repeating.

Edwin Booth's brother was twenty-six when he jumped onto the stage at Ford's Theatre, wild-eyed, spewing nonsense in Latin. When *I* was twenty-six, I jumped onto the stage of the Lyric Theatre, wild-eyed and spewing Italian. At twenty-seven, I was spewing French and German. By the time I was twenty-nine, I was simply spewing.

My opera plan had worked. But like all my plans, it had not worked in the way I'd intended. I'd gotten my AGMA card and my SAG card and started auditioning for union commercials that paid actual money. But I had not quit the opera as planned. I had stayed on—because Mike Gellert had been correct. The music was terrific. The orchestra was world class. The chorus girls turned out to be friendly. Very friendly. By 1990, I'd sung in nearly two dozen productions and even had a few solo lines. My Italian had gotten no better, but I had ingratiated myself into the fabric of the chorus and become a useful, if not entirely reliable, participant.

One evening, during the intermission of something in German, Gellert and I slipped out the stage door and walked over to the Mount Royal Tavern for a couple of beers and a few minutes of the football game. We were dressed like Vikings, but the patrons of the Mount Royal Tavern were in no way surprised; they had seen us in a variety of costumes over the years, always during the intermission of some opera.

Gellert and I took our usual seats at the bar. But when we looked up at the TV, the game was not on. Instead, we saw a fat man in a shiny suit selling pots and pans.

"What the hell, Rick? Where's the game?"

"It's halftime," the bartender said.

"Okay. But why are we watching a fat man in a shiny suit selling pots and pans?"

"Because I'm auditioning for his job tomorrow and I'm trying to figure out what that guy does, exactly."

It was the first time I'd ever seen or heard of QVC.

Rick explained it to me: The network was basically a twenty-four-hour commercial and currently engaged in a nationwide talent search. It had come to Baltimore and was holding a cattle-call audition the next morning over at the Marriott in the Inner Harbor. As he poured us another beer, Gellert nodded to the TV and said, "I bet you could do that."

"What?" I said. "Get fat and dress like a used-car salesman?"

"You keep saying you want to work in television. That looks like television to me. You should audition."

"Last time you told me to audition for something, I wound up in a bar dressed like a Viking, watching an infomercial."

"You're welcome," he said.

"Laugh all you want," said Rick, nodding toward the screen. "That fat guy in the shiny suit makes $200,000 a year. Starting salary is $60,000, plus a bonus."

We drank our beer and continued to watch QVC. The thought of a twenty-four-hour commercial struck me as a sign of the apocalypse. A harbinger of doom. An end to Western civilization. That or a steady paycheck—something I had yet to experience in my chosen field.

We got back to the Lyric in time to make our entrance, spew some German, and take our bows. But that night in bed, I flicked around the dial and found QVC. I watched a nervous-looking woman try to sell me a treadmill, a simulated diamond bracelet, and an eel-skin handbag.

Amazing.

I drifted off with the TV still on. When I got up to pee, I saw a sweaty gentleman in a leisure suit hawking unbreakable plates and stemware, followed by an electronic device that purported to keep mosquitos away.

$60,000 a year? Plus a bonus?

The next morning, I drove downtown to the Marriott. There, as you know, I talked about a pencil for eight minutes straight and landed my first job in television—the job that taught me "submissive posture," among other things. What you don't know is that I wound up forgetting the important lessons I learned on that job. For many years, I went out of my way to forget them. Later on, I'll tell you about those years, too—a time I think of today as my years in the woods. A time that lasted until I found a path that led me to the place I should have been all along.

THE AMERICAN ROCK STAR

The toilet had never done anything to Jason. Nevertheless, Jason was determined to blow it to pieces.

His reasons were those of a moody kid plagued with enough teenage angst to fill the entire state of Washington. So Jason lit the fuse of the M-80, dropped it into the bowl, closed the lid, and walked out of the restroom. A minute later, the toilet was gone, as a deafening roar echoed through the hallways of his junior high school.

Today, a stunt like that would have landed Jason in jail. Luckily, that was the early 1980s, and the school principal decided on a week's suspension instead. Luckier still was Jason's grandmother's decision to take the boy to one of the most expensive psychiatrists in the state. And luckiest of all was the presence of several guitars in the psychiatrist's office.

Jason didn't have much to say to the shrink. And so the psychiatrist invited him to pick up a guitar and start strumming. Before long, the two were jamming their way through their scheduled sessions, launching what his grandmother would later call "the most expensive guitar lessons in the world." By the time he had finished high school, he still had some angst, but he also had a plan: Jason was going to be a rock star.

His first band made a splash in the Seattle grunge scene. They showed real potential. But there was something in Jason that still wanted to blow things up, and that time it wasn't the plumbing—it was the opportunity. Jason became difficult to work with and even less fun to be around. His friends and family watched in horror as the promising band was forced, however reluctantly, to replace him.

But destiny wasn't quite done with Jason. After some genuine regret and self-reflection, the rock star in waiting was given a second chance. This time, a band of older, more established musicians saw his undeniable talent and welcomed him into the fold. Overnight, Jason was playing to sold-out arenas, standing ovations, and glowing reviews from everyone. But again, he couldn't seem to handle the success he thought he craved.

Was he depressed? Or just depressing to be around? Whatever the case, he retreated into himself once again—and his reluctant bandmates had no choice but to replace him.

Sometimes, when you hit what feels like the bottom, it's not enough to simply start over. Sometimes you need to go in a completely different direction. So Jason did something most aspiring rock stars don't do: He cut his hair. He lost the nose ring. He enlisted in the army and applied for a fast-track program into Ranger School.

Not only did Jason get in—he excelled.

From Fort Benning, Georgia, it was off to Fort Lewis, Washington—not far from where he had blown up that innocent toilet ten years earlier. There he completed his Ranger training and got a round-trip ticket to Latin America, where he fought in a number of covert drug wars. Then it was off to Asia to fight piracy on the high seas.

Jason served with distinction but he wanted more. At twenty-six, he applied for the Special Forces and got in, completing his final phase of training on September 11, 2001. In no time, he was up to his neck in the world's most dangerous places. In Afghanistan, he smelled the poppy fields of Kandahar, came face-to-face with suicide bombers, and learned the local language. He helicoptered in for midnight raids and fought on horseback. In Iraq, he fired grenades from a Humvee in front of the front line of America's biggest conventional military operation since World War II.

Jason was back on the stage now—the world stage—playing with a very different kind of band: a band of brothers.

You won't get the details from Jason. Most of what he did is still classified. But the medals and photos covering the wall in the cabin he calls home today are both numerous and hard to discount. The coveted Combat Infantryman Badge sits next to a photo of Jason with Donald Rumsfeld and General Stanley McChrystal. You might say that in blowing things up, he finally found a career he couldn't destroy. And by hitting the reset button when he did, he did something rather extraordinary.

Because while Jason is certainly not the only musician to sabotage his own career, he might be the only one to do so in such spectacular, incomparable fashion. If you thought that Pete Best blew his chance with the Beatles, consider this: the first band Jason bungled sold 30 million records in a single year—the year after he got himself fired.

Thirty million.

And the second band? Don't even get me started on the second band, which outlasted the first one.

Ultimately, Jason Everman, the guitar player everyone wanted, missed out on more than 100 million albums sold—and many, many millions of dollars. What he wound up with was a hell of a story. The story of a guy who washed out of Nirvana *and* Soundgarden, but still went on to become . . . an American rock star.

Back when Jason was dressed in camouflage, shooting Taliban, I was dressed in wrinkle-free rayon, shooting infomercials. But I did wear a uniform once: olive green regalia with short pants, knee socks, and a long sash festooned with a few dozen merit badges. It was during my time in that uniform that I, too, lit a fuse. Like Jason, I came close to blowing up my own future.

In 1976, my scoutmaster was a retired army colonel who treated the boys in his troop—Troop 16—like recruits. *His* recruits. Mr. Huntington divided us into five separate "patrols" and put me in charge of one called "The Trailblazers." Patrol leaders reported to the senior patrol leader, who reported to the assistant scoutmaster, who reported to the scoutmaster. That chain of command was designed to teach us respect for authority. A scout is obedient, after all.

Rick Hansen was in my patrol. He was a frail, pale kid cursed with a serious stutter. Not a minor stammer, like the one I had in those days. A full-on, world-class, Porky Pig–style speech impediment. It was so severe that he seldom spoke. But one day in school, during our ninth-grade science class, Ricky surprised us. Our teacher, Mr. Tubbs, asked us if we knew what "Au" stood for on the periodic table of elements. Rick raised his hand—an unprecedented gesture.

"Yes, Ricky? Tell us the answer."

"Is it guh-guh . . . guh-guh . . . guh-guh . . . ?"

It was hard to watch. It was even harder to listen to. I wanted to say it for him—"It's gold, Ricky, gold!"—but I also wanted him to say it for himself.

He never got a chance to.

"What is 'guh-guh'?" Mr. Tubbs asked. "Can somebody please tell me what 'guh-guh' means?"

The class laughed, Ricky turned red, and I felt a kind of anger I'd never felt before. A righteous anger that made my ears ring and my fists clench. In a roomful of children, Mr. Tubbs himself had behaved like a child. A cruel child. Something had to be done. But what? What was justice for Rick Hansen going to look like?

I had an idea. Later that day, while Mr. Tubbs was sitting alone at his desk, reading *Sports Illustrated*, I lit the fuse of an M-80 smoke bomb and slid it under his door.

The classroom filled up in seconds with thick yellow smoke—the kind of smoke a pilot could have seen from 5,000 feet. Mr. Tubbs bolted straight out of the classroom, the smoke followed him into the hallway, the entire school was evacuated, and within a few minutes, fire engines arrived. Most of the smoke had dissipated by then, along with most of my anger. At which point my thoughts turned to a more pressing matter: Would I get away with it?

That question was answered almost as soon as Mr. Tubbs got on the school intercom and offered a $20 reward to anyone who could identify "the perpetrator of this heinous act."

Before an hour had passed, a toady—let's call him Kevin, since that was his name—had ratted me out. Down at the principal's office, Mr. Tubbs made his case for my expulsion, a request the principal said he'd consider. In the meantime, I was to be suspended until further notice.

I couldn't believe I'd done what I'd done. I didn't know what I would tell my father, who was a public school teacher himself. For a few hours, I pretended that nothing had happened. Walking through Double Rock Park, as I always did after school, I arrived at the Maryland School for the Blind, where I had been working on my Eagle Scout project. It occurred to me as I walked that I might be mentally ill. Seriously, how many aspiring Eagle Scouts get themselves expelled for throwing smoke bombs at their teachers? A scout is helpful, after all. Who exactly had I helped with that act of terrorism?

My dad sensed right away that something was wrong.

"Is there something on your mind, Michael?" he asked as he drove me home later that day.

"Well, Dad," I said, "I threw a smoke bomb into Mr. Tubbs's classroom today. The school was evacuated. I've been suspended indefinitely."

My father cocked his head and stared at me in much the same way as a cow might regard a new gate. "Have you lost your mind?" he asked.

"It's possible," I said. "I thought of that, too. But I had a good reason."

My father didn't speak again until we were parked in front of the house. Then he turned to me and simply asked, "Why?"

"Mr. Tubbs made fun of Rick Hansen's stutter," I said.

Dad lit his pipe and told me to go tell my mother. She, too, looked at me incredulously. She congratulated me on ruining my life. Then she told me to go feed the horses.

I didn't sleep that night, but the next morning Dad drove me to school and somehow made things better. Whatever he said to the principal worked: I got off with a stern warning and a week of detention, which was rescinded when my father pointed out that I worked with the blind after school.

I'd dodged a bullet—no punishment at school and no punishment at home—while Kevin was ostracized for ratting me out. He became known as "Kevin the Fink," and Ricky Hansen was grateful, even though it took him several minutes to actually articulate his gratitude. There was one more anxious moment afterward: Sounding every bit like the colonel he'd been, Mr. Huntington called me in front of the troop, chewed me out, and told me that I had behaved "precipitously," with no respect for my future, public safety, or authority.

"Worst of all," he said, "*you showed no respect for the uniform!*"

Then he winked and told me to get back into line . . . where I've tried to remain ever since.

THE 25-MILLION-DOLLAR KISS

Hedwig was beautiful and married to a man she didn't love. Fritz was an arms merchant and deeply possessive of his trophy wife.

At their home in Austria, Hedwig was a fly on the wall at more than a few dinner parties, listening quietly as important men discussed with her husband evolving technologies that would change the complexion of modern warfare. Fritz's guests were intelligent and influential. Some were physicists. Some were inventors. Many were fascists. Many were Nazis.

Hedwig didn't care for fascists, or Nazis. She didn't like them in her house or at her table—and she hated the fact that her husband was selling them weapons. And so, as one more dinner party approached, Hedwig selected from her vast wardrobe the most glamorous evening gown that she could find. She adorned herself with every piece of expensive jewelry she owned. She smiled sweetly during the appetizer and listened attentively during the main course. Just before dessert, she went off to powder her nose. She never returned.

The next morning, a stunning woman arrived in Paris by train. After that, it was your basic Hollywood fairy tale: Hedwig Eva

Maria Kiesler was "discovered" by the movie mogul Louis B. Mayer. A year later, she was starring opposite Clark Gable. By then, she had a new name to go with her new address in Hollywood. By 1941, she was widely regarded as the most beautiful woman in the world.

In fact, Hedwig was so gorgeous that she was deemed "too beautiful to speak"—and was given very little dialogue on the big screen. Once, when asked to explain the secret of being glamorous, Hedwig said, "That's easy. All you have to do is stand still and look stupid."

But Hedwig wasn't stupid. Far from it. Among other things, she was an amateur inventor—a woman who spent most of her free time at home hunched over her drafting table. Her big idea was a thing she'd been tinkering with in response to the Germans, who were targeting cruise ships in the Atlantic, murdering hundreds of civilians.

Hedwig had read that the Allies were unable to sink German U-boats because the Germans had figured out how to jam the torpedos' radio frequencies. She recalled a scientist at one of those dinner parties in Vienna. He had been talking to Fritz about the untapped potential of radio waves in the context of modern warfare.

Now Hedwig wondered, "What if a single radio signal could hop randomly from one frequency to another? How would the Nazis block *that*?"

The question was ingenious, and so was the answer.

She developed the technology, patented it, and offered it to the navy free of charge. But the US military had a hard time believing the most beautiful woman in the world had come up with the solution to a problem that they themselves hadn't been able to solve. The navy wasn't interested in her idea. In fact, Hedwig was told that if she really wanted to help the war effort, she would need to use the assets for which she was best known.

Hedwig was disappointed, but she knew that she did have the assets in question, and she was eager to contribute—to help, in any way, to win the war. So, to raise money for war bonds, she began selling kisses. In a single night, she raised $7 million—just by "standing still and looking stupid." Over time, she raised $25 million. In today's money, that's more than $220 million.

If the story had ended right here, it still would have made a good headline: "The most beautiful girl in the world fights off Nazis with kisses!" But Hedwig's story was far from over. During a very anxious week in 1962, known as the Cuban Missile Crisis, her technology was finally employed—and it worked. Big-time.

Hedwig was given no thanks or acknowledgment. Nor did she ask for any. But let's be absolutely clear about the enormity of the idea she had patented: Not only did "radio hopping" change the face of national security; it led directly to the development of our modern-day satellite communications system, and a handy bit of technology we know as "Wi-Fi." Without her invention, I could have never researched her life at 37,000 feet and shared her story with you—the story of a beautiful girl who knew which assets mattered most. A movie star named . . . Hedy Lamarr.

I'm twelve years old, sitting in a darkened theater with my eighteen-year-old cousin, who has smuggled me into my first R-rated movie. On the screen, a group of cowboys are huddled around a campfire. They're finishing their evening meal when one of them farts. I'm not sure how to react, and neither, it seems, are the adults around me. That sort of thing happened in the Boy Scouts all the time, but uninhibited farting on the big screen? It was so unexpected.

Moments after the first fart, another fart follows, and another fart after that. Soon all of the men around the campfire are farting and I'm dying—laughing nervously at first and then so much that it hurts. As the grown-ups around me begin to laugh, too, my mirth escalates ever further. So does my cousin's. The more the men fart, the harder we laugh—and the men don't stop farting. Soon tears run down our faces, and I can feel the Junior Mints in my belly threatening a hasty exit. Grown-ups laughing at the sound of other grown-ups farting? This is simply unprecedented.

The movie was *Blazing Saddles*, and the first time I saw it I laughed through the entire thing. I laughed when Alex Karras punched the horse. I laughed when Cleavon Little asked, "Where all the white women at?" I even laughed at jokes I didn't get. I very nearly peed myself when Hedley Lamarr, played to perfection by Harvey Korman, became more and more exasperated over people's tendency to call him "Hedy."

"It's *Hedley*," he said over and over again. "Not Hedy, *Hedley!*"

Why is this so funny? I have no idea. It just is. I ask my cousin who Hedy Lamarr is, but he's laughing too hard to answer. He laughs so hard a snot bubble explodes from his left nostril—and that sends me into another spasm of uncontrollable giggling. Before long, we're both on our hands and knees, gasping for breath, laughing ourselves sick for reasons we can't even articulate—and every time that we think we've recovered, Harvey Korman says the magic words that set us off again: "Not Hedy, *Hedley!*"

When I get home, I tell my father about this hysterical character, Hedley Lamarr.

"Not Hedley," he says. "Hedy."

"Wait, what? There's a real person called Hedy Lamarr?"

"Sure," he says. "Hedy Lamarr is the most beautiful woman in the world."

"Really? Do you have a picture?"

"No," my mother yells from the kitchen. "Your father doesn't have a picture of Hedy Lamarr!"

My father turns back to his newspaper, neither confirming nor denying.

"What does she look like?" I ask.

"She looks like your mother," he says, a little louder than necessary. "Now go split some wood. You'll feel better."

Out in the garden, ax in hand, I still have questions. Why don't I know who the most beautiful girl in the world is? How can I be twelve years old and still be so . . . uninformed?

Today I'd google her and see for myself. But back then, Hedy's ingenious invention had not yet led to the development of Wi-Fi. So

I had to wait until Monday, when I could avail myself of the services of our county library. There, under a fog of disapproval emanating from the librarian who assisted me, I perused a stack of books about Hollywood starlets from days gone by.

There she was: Hedy Lamarr.

Wow! She was indeed "a looker," as my grandfather would say. Sure enough, the caption identified Hedy as "the most beautiful woman in the world." It gave the date and the place of her birth. But there was no mention of anything else, except for lists of the films she'd appeared in and the men she had dated. And so, aside from that random reference in *Blazing Saddles*, that was the only thing that I'd know about Hedy Lamarr until I *did* google her, forty-five years later at 37,000 feet. Only then did I learn about the person she really had been—or at least the person the internet says she was.

Quick digression: My friend Alex is a wreck of a man but one heck of a writer. He dropped by the other day to see how this book was coming along.

"You tell me," I said, handing him a stack of pages.

Alex claims to know what he's doing, and there's evidence to suggest he might be right. After reading a couple of chapters, he stopped. "If you do this right," he said, "there'll come a time when your book starts talking to you. When that happens, you should listen."

I didn't know what he was talking about. Fish don't fly. Books don't talk. Then again, maybe they do. So, I'm beginning to wonder if any of these stories are all the way finished. Consider the very first one in the book: the one about Mel Brooks.

When I started it, I wanted to pay tribute to the man who'd made me laugh harder than I'd ever laughed before. With the help of Hedy Lamarr's invention, I googled him and learned that, once upon a time, the man who wrote, directed, and starred in the funniest movie I've ever seen had climbed a utility pole in the Ardennes, hooked up a loudspeaker, and played a song by a Jewish singer to a forest filled with Nazis. That struck me as a story worth sharing. Picture him there, up at the top of that pole. The moon is out. The woods are full of Nazi sharpshooters. And there's Brooks: he might as well have a bull's-eye on his back, and he's doing it all for a joke. That's brave and brilliant and also dumb. Smart-stupid, like most of his movies. As I pictured the scene, I saw the same sensibility that informed every frame of *Blazing Saddles*—the movie that led me to Hedy Lamarr. Googling her (thanks to Mel Brooks), I learned that this "most beautiful woman in the world" was also a brilliant inventor. That struck me as a story worth sharing for a number of reasons, chief among them the undeniable fact that I wouldn't have been able to write these stories without her invention.

Maybe this was what Alex was talking about? Maybe here the book was talking back—and what it was telling me sounded a lot like "Keep digging."

And so I did, and late last night, I learned that Hedy Lamarr sued Mel Brooks when *Blazing Saddles* came out. She was upset that her name—or something close to it—was being used without her permission.

I guess I can't really blame her. Hedy's first husband treated her like an object. The studios treated her like horseflesh. The US government treated her like a punk. Maybe she'd had enough. Maybe the thought of people laughing at the mention of her name—or something close to it—was too much to bear.

Here's the kicker, though: Mel Brooks would have prevailed in court. In fact, he could have *countersued* Hedy and won. But guess what he did instead? He paid her. The funniest man in the world wrote a check to the most beautiful woman in the world because, as he put it, "She's given us so much."

"Pay her whatever she needs," Brooks said. "Send her my love, and tell her where I live."

The interview's out there, online. You can see it for yourself. Go ahead, google it.

I'll wait.

HOW THE GAME WAS PLAYED

Saul Venzor had pitched himself into a jam. After eight scoreless innings, he'd begun the ninth by giving up two hits and a walk. Now the bases were loaded with no outs, and Saul was cursing the umpire over a ball that should have been a strike:

"*Puta ciega!*"

In those days, you could call the umpire a blind whore. That's how the game was played.

Saul stepped off the mound, grabbed a handful of dirt, and twisted the baseball between his giant hands. In the stands, his handicapped nephew watched his every move. Saul caught his nephew's eye and gave him a wink. *No problemo.* Then he turned his attention to the visitors' dugout, where the members of the opposing team were shouting encouragements at their batter: "Wait for your pitch, Alejandro. He's got nothing! Little man, little arm."

But there was nothing little about the six-foot-five pitcher. Everything about Saul was big, including his ego.

"*Hora!*" Saul yelled. The umpire raised both arms and called, "Time!"

Saul's nephew watched his uncle stroll toward the opposing dugout and address the now silent players.

"Five dollars says I end this game without giving up a single run.
Any takers?"

In those days, in the minor leagues, you could make friendly
wagers. That's how the game was played.

The men on the opposing team weren't flush with cash. Like
Saul, they were all migrant workers. But the odds were too good to
resist. They pooled their money. They made their wager. Then they
watched in horror as Saul struck out the side. Final score: Santa Bar-
bara Merchants, 1; Oxnard Aces, 0.

It was one of many moments that Saul's nephew would never
forget. Maybe not as dramatic as the exhibition game in which his
uncle had struck out Babe Ruth or the time he'd pitched nineteen
consecutive innings in a legendary duel against the minor-league
team from Los Angeles. But memorable nonetheless, because the
events of that day gave the boy a close look at the very qualities *he'd*
need to shape his own career: a potent mix of raw talent, supreme
confidence, and boundless machismo.

Many years later, after setting records that remain unbroken to
this day, Saul's nephew would recall the long driveway on Chino
Street where his uncle had shown him his ninety-mile-an-hour
fastball—up close and personal. Saul was not the kind of uncle who'd
let you win just to build up your confidence. Nor was he inclined to
cut you any slack just because you were born with certain . . . dis-
advantages. No: Saul Venzor was the uncle who teased and taunted.
The uncle who sent you home in tears and dared you to come back
for more, if you had the *cojones.*

In those days, there were no participation trophies. That's how
the game was played.

Saul's nephew liked to come to Chino Street because there, no
one cared about his handicap. There, a kid like him could learn to
hit a major-league fastball. There, a kid like him could learn how to

be a man. Thanks to the things that his uncle had taught him, Saul's nephew was drafted to a minor-league team straight out of high school. By the time he was twenty-one, he was playing in the majors. By the end of his rookie year, everyone was talking about the Latin Legend: a baseball prodigy who'd hit .327, with 31 home runs and a league-leading 145 RBIs.

Well—sort of. The stats are correct. The chatter *was* exceedingly complimentary. But no one was talking about "the Latin Legend"—because no one knew that Saul's nephew was Hispanic. You see, the boy's mother had married a gringo. The boy had inherited

his father's complexion, along with his distinctly American name. And in 1939—eight years before Jackie Robinson broke baseball's color barrier—that was a very handy thing. Handy because guys like Saul and his nephew were handicapped by their ethnicity. The Negro League was a thing in those days, and the Mexicans—they had a league of their own, as well.

In those days, that's how the game was played.

Make no mistake, Saul's nephew knew how to play that game. He concealed his handicap for his entire career, and when he was inducted into the Hall of Fame in 1966, he acknowledged all of his coaches, from high school on up to the majors. He acknowledged his manager, along with the owner of the Red Sox, his teammates, and all the sportswriters who'd voted for him. The only name he didn't mention was the name of the man whose ethnicity would have revealed his own. That of his Mexican uncle. The man who had taught him how to play the game.

It's hard to know how to feel about that. Some people say that if Saul's nephew had embraced his "handicap," he might have paved the way for other Mexican-American players. Others say that doing so would have kept him out of the majors, dooming him to a career as obscure as his uncle's had been. I guess we'll never know. But this much we *do* know: thirty-six years after his election to the National Baseball Hall of Fame, the eighty-three-year-old left fielder who'd kept his Mexican heritage a secret became the first inductee into the Hispanic Heritage Baseball Museum Hall of Fame. A seventeen-time All-Star, the last man to bat over .400—the greatest hitter of all time, in fact. That was Saul Venzor's nephew. A devastating athlete with Mexican roots who'd concealed his true heritage throughout his career.

The great baseball player you know as . . . Ted Williams.

I got to meet Ted Williams once, the night before QVC fired me for the third and final time. I didn't actually interview him; Dan Wheeler was the go-to host for anything baseball related. Celebrities didn't appear on the graveyard shift. But I came in early that night to watch from the greenroom and, hopefully, shake the man's hand after the show.

It was a good show. Wheeler asked Williams how he'd do batting against modern-day pitching greats.

"I don't know," Williams said. "Pitchers today are throwing at a whole other level. I guess maybe I'd hit .270. Maybe .275."

Dan was aghast. ".270? No way! You? The greatest hitter who ever lived?"

"Well," Williams said, "you gotta remember—I'm seventy-three years old!"

Mickey Mantle called in. Just to chat. Ted talked to him as though they were on opposite sides of a crowded bar.

"HEY MICK, HOW THEY HANGIN'? I STOPPED

BY YOUR RESTAURANT A FEW MONTHS AGO! YOU WEREN'T THERE!! HAD A PRETTY GOOD STEAK, THOUGH!!!"

I could hear screams from the audio booth, Dan Wheeler fell off his chair, as baseball fans across the nation lurched for the volume buttons on their remotes.

Afterward, Ted came up to the greenroom. He looked tired, a bit pale.

"Nice job, Mr. Williams," I said. "You're a natural."

Ted Williams smiled, sort of. Then he glanced at the monitor, where Dan Wheeler was segueing into his upcoming hour of plus-sized fashions: "Hey, ladies, let's say you're going on a cruise . . ."

"Thanks," Williams said. "But there's nothing natural about any of this."

"You want to see something unnatural? Stick around until three in the morning. I've got an hour of collectible dolls coming up."

"You're shitting me," Williams said.

"No, sir. I don't joke about collectible dolls."

Williams looked at me like I was an umpire who'd just blown a call.

"Seriously?" he said. "People really collect dolls?"

"People collect everything, Mr. Williams."

"Maybe I'll watch from my hotel room," he said.

"Nothing unnatural about that," I told him.

Williams laughed and, in that instant, I saw the great athlete for who he was: a mortal man who'd come to QVC for the same reason that I had.

He had come for the money.

This was back in 1993. I thought about money a lot in those days. Specifically, about how nice it was to finally have some. I'd always sensed that the ice at QVC was thin beneath my feet, so I had saved every penny, knowing my next paycheck could be my last. Living rent free at Georgia Farm had been a big help. My father's parsimony, which I had inherited, had instilled in me a pathological fear of debt—neither a borrower nor a lender be, and all that. And so, with the help of my trusted financial adviser—a man I'd come to think of as my friend—I had managed to accumulate a tidy nest egg. But meeting Ted Williams made me wonder how big a nest egg I'd need. If the greatest hitter of all time had to drag his ass to West Chester, Pennsylvania, to hawk autographed baseballs on a home shopping network, what would I be doing when I was his age?

That troubling question became more acute the next day, when I learned that QVC no longer required my services. Apparently, my interactions the night before with a shapely Victorian lady named "Rebecca" had crossed a line. When I got the news, I didn't panic or think about my future. I thought about Ted Williams.

Had he watched my final moments on air from the comfort of his hotel room? Had he been sipping a brandy as I spilled my guts to that collectible doll—sharing with her my disappointment with past girlfriends, along with the thousand natural shocks that flesh is heir to?

Had he laughed when I wondered aloud if "a guy like me would have a shot with a doll" like her?

I sure hope so. I hope Ted Williams doubled over when I held Rebecca like a microphone and sang "I Won't Send Roses" into her pretty, pinched porcelain face. I like to picture him laughing and snorting and wondering out loud, to no one in particular—"Are you shitting me?"—before settling back in bed to sleep and, perchance, to dream.

Now, *that* would be a consummation devoutly to be wished.

THE MYSTERY OF
THE VANISHING WOMAN

The woman checked into the resort alone. She arrived without reservations or luggage. She signed the guest book as Miss Neele and said she was visiting from Cape Town, South Africa, 8,500 miles to the south.

For the next twenty-four hours, Miss Neele kept a low profile. Then a sharp-eyed banjo player recognized her from a photo in the paper. The banjo player knew that there was a reward for her apprehension. He called the authorities immediately. Moments later, detectives were on their way from London, hoping Miss Neele might help resolve a missing persons case unlike any other.

The investigation had started two weeks earlier, when a car was found on a steep incline near a former rock quarry called the Silent Pool. The car's windshield was cracked. The headlights were still on. Inside the police found a suitcase, a fur coat, and a driver's license belonging to one of the most recognizable women in England. Given the woman's wealth, detectives had feared a possible kidnapping—but there was no ransom note. They had questioned dozens of people, including the woman's husband. He feared that his wife might have killed herself.

"She's been in a terrible state," Archie said. "Ever since her mother's death, she's been deeply depressed. It's been quite terrible."

The police tossed pronged hooks on ropes into the Silent Pool and dragged for a body. Bloodhounds were deployed. Fifteen thousand volunteers swept the countryside from Guildford to London. For the first time ever, airplanes were employed to search for a missing person. Arthur Conan Doyle—the creator of Sherlock Holmes—paid for the services of a medium. But no luck.

England's newspapers couldn't get enough of the mystery.

"A Suicide with No Corpse!" the headlines blared.

"A Murder with No Suspects!"

"A Kidnapping with No Ransom!"

Across the pond in New York, the *Times* covered the mystery on its front page with a headline that read simply, "Who Done It?" But "Who done it?" wasn't the question—not really. The real question was "What happened?"

How could a woman as famous as that just vanish from the face of the Earth?

Then Scotland Yard started to crack the case. Detectives there learned that Archie had asked for a divorce a month earlier—a request his missing wife had refused. Interesting. They also learned that Archie stood to inherit a great deal of money if his wife never returned. That was interesting, too. It gave them a motive, but, alas— Archie had an alibi. On the night of his wife's vanishing he'd been at a dinner party with several people, all of whom vouched for his presence. Then there was another break in the case: one of the witnesses turned out to be Archie's young secretary—a young secretary who, it turned out, was having an affair with Archie. A young secretary named—that's right—Miss Neele.

Archie admitted the affair immediately, but even after prolonged questioning, he insisted that he had no knowledge regarding the whereabouts of his missing wife. At which point the detectives turned their attention to Miss Neele. What did the young secretary have to say to the detectives about the mysterious disappearance of the woman whose husband she loved? Clearly, this was a woman who needed to be interrogated. And so, she was.

Detectives converged on the quiet resort in North Yorkshire. Inside, the band played as guests danced and dined. The banjo player saw them and nodded in the direction of the dining room—and that's where they found "Miss Neele," chatting with a few other guests over a game of bridge. Only the Miss Neele they found was not Archie's mistress. Nor was she Archie's secretary. Nor was she from South Africa. This Miss Neele had no ID, no memory of how she had gotten to the hotel, and no idea why she had identified herself as Miss Neele. But even though *this* Miss Neele didn't know who she was, the detectives most assuredly did. She was the woman on the front page of every newspaper in Great Britain. She was the elusive subject of what had been the largest manhunt in English history. Now she had finally been found, safe and sound and happy as a lark, 240 miles from her home, at a hotel where she had checked in under the name of her husband's lover. But why? Thus began the *real* Mystery of the Vanishing Woman.

"For twenty-four hours," the woman said, "I wandered in a dream, and then found myself in Harrogate as a well-contented and perfectly happy woman who believed she had just come from South Africa."

Doctors said that she had entered a "fugue state" brought on by stress. In such a condition, they said, a person could black out while remaining fully conscious. But when the story hit the papers, it begged more questions than it answered: How could the woman have gone unrecognized for so long when the entire country had been looking for her? She must have known about Archie's affair with the real Miss Neele. Was her disappearance an attempt to shame the philandering husband? Had the husband drugged her, perhaps to declare her insane and steal all of her money? Or was it all a publicity stunt—a promotion for her latest book?

Everyone had a theory, but no one had a clue.

Once she had been brought back home, Archie's soon-to-be ex-wife quickly regained her senses. She divorced the husband, who immediately married his secretary—the real Miss Neele. Then she left her home once again. This time she left the car in her garage, hopped a train to Baghdad, and had an exotic journey she'd never forget: a trip where she found adventure, inspiration, and new love. By the time she died, many years later, at the ripe old age of eighty-five, the woman who'd been at the center of England's largest manhunt was happily married, more famous than ever, and the best-selling author of all time.

But here's an odd thing: of all the mysteries that surrounded this remarkable woman, the true tale of her strange vanishing is largely forgotten. It might be because, after returning from her trip to Baghdad, she refused to discuss the matter again. Even her autobiography makes no mention of the incident. In fact, her bizarre disappearance in 1926 is the only unsolved mystery in her compendium of tantalizing whodunits—sixty-six in all, written by a heartbroken wife who found a fresh start on the Orient Express, bound for Baghdad. A woman known, very briefly, as Miss Neele, who is best known today as a Dame named . . . Agatha Christie.

Twenty-one mysteries of Georgia Farm revealed themselves to me all at once in 1991, while I was snowbound and trying to stay sane. I stumbled across them in Morris Stroud's study: a stack of dog-eared paperbacks by John D. MacDonald. Each one had a color in its title: *Bright Orange for the Shroud*, *A Deadly Shade of Gold*, *Pale Gray for Guilt*, *The Quick Red Fox*, and so forth. The first in the series—*The Deep Blue Good-by*—was the best pulp fiction I'd ever read. More importantly, it was the book that introduced me to Travis McGee.

McGee is a combat veteran turned salvage expert—a man who specializes in recovering that which has been conned or swindled from people who can't turn to the police for help. He's a modern-day knight-errant who lives in Florida on a houseboat called the *Busted Flush*. McGee works when he wants to, takes only the cases that interest him, and answers to no one. He isn't cheap—half of all he recovers he keeps for himself—but he always delivers. He always gets the girl. He always does something admirable along the way. To this day, I talk about McGee in the present tense; I like to believe he's still down there in Bahia Mar, sleeping on the *Busted Flush*, sipping Boodles gin, waiting for the next damaged soul in need of assistance to come knocking.

For a guy living in a haunted mansion, McGee was great company. For a guy stuck on the graveyard shift at QVC, he was nothing short of inspirational. I read every book in the series and found myself yearning to live like my fictitious friend. Not on a houseboat, necessarily, or as a salvage expert, per se, but as an inveterate freelancer, unencumbered by unnecessary obligations. Thanks to McGee, I started to question the wisdom of working at any one place for any one boss. And so, when QVC fired me once and for all, I began auditioning only for those projects that seemed doomed to fail. Ones that would not tie me up for more than a few months at a time.

To my delight, opportunities were everywhere.

Joan Rivers provided the first with that QVC/CBS hybrid *Can We Shop?*—a rhetorical question whose answer turned out to be a very literal "no." It was canceled after three episodes, but no one blamed me. In fact, I was praised for my performance and quickly hired to host *Romantic Escapes*—a Discovery show that turned out to be neither one of those things. It was canceled after the first season, but again, I wasn't blamed. I was hired to host *New York Expeditions* for PBS, *The Most* for the History Channel, and *Bodysense*, a syndicated program sponsored by *Prevention* magazine, with a weekly audience of dozens. I also hosted *Worst-Case Scenario*, a breathtakingly unwatchable TBS show that lived up to its name in every conceivable way. But was I concerned?

I was not. I'd had a revelation: I could make real money by hosting shows that no one watched. My favorite failure was an empty shell of a show that aired exclusively at 37,000 feet. American Airlines needed stuff that, in its words, "looked like content."

On Air TV, it was called.

As the host, I was given a pass that allowed me to fly first-class to any destination American served, then make a show about that location. But when I say "show," I don't mean a TV show. I mean a piece of fluff designed to surround commercials specifically produced for American's captive audiences. Basically, it was an airborne infomercial that took me all over the United States. But the pass also took me to Sydney, Cape Town, Amsterdam, and other exotic places—because, coincidentally (or maybe not), that "magic ticket" stayed active for several years after *On Air TV* had been canceled.

This happy oversight I neglected to bring to the airline's attention. A Scout is thrifty, after all.

Point is, all of those projects paid a fair wage for a few months of my time. Better yet, they gave me the freedom to audition for other kinds of work: commercials, industrial films, narration, voice-overs. I even did some modeling work. There I was, standing in my underwear in a Boscov's catalog holding a football, pretending to throw it—presumably to another thirty-two-year-old man in *his* underwear standing on some other page. I didn't know if I was selling footballs or underpants, but I didn't care. I got paid.

I auditioned for Domino's, too. They were introducing a new deep-dish pizza and wanted a low voice for the ad campaign: "Looking for a James Earl Jones quality." I channeled Darth Vader as I read the copy: "When it's gotta be deep and it's gotta be thick," I said in my deepest basso profundo, "it's gotta be Domino's." Amazingly, I got the gig—and ended up with fifty thousand dollars in residuals.

Can you imagine? Fifty grand, for one silly line. The checks arrived that summer in $800 increments, filling my mailbox with thousands of dollars, week after week. I had seen the light. Voice-overs were my secret weapon. Residuals, my salvation.

Travis McGee kept his stash hidden in the bow of his boat, but I knew better. I sent my earnings to the trusted financial adviser I'd come to think of as my friend and built up my nest egg—a respectable safety net that allowed me to start taking my retirement in early installments, just like Travis McGee. Do I sound proud of myself? Well, I was. While most of my friends in the industry were swinging for the fences—struggling to get that big hit—I concentrated on singles. Singles that paid off in spades. By 2002, I had a financial portfolio worth north of a million dollars. I didn't own much more than a toothbrush, lived in hotels, worked eight months of the year on projects I didn't care about, and took full and complete advantage of my magical American Airlines ticket. I was thirty-seven years old and delightfully unencumbered—until the day a letter arrived, informing me that the trusted financial adviser I'd come to think of as my friend had been running a massive Ponzi scheme with his clients' money. It was a betrayal unlike anything I had ever experienced.

Overnight, I lost everything. The safety net I had constructed was gone, and Travis McGee was nowhere to be found . . .

HIS LAST LETTER HOME

The postman snapped the rubber band off the envelopes and slid another stack of mail through the slot in the front door. Ingrid heard the squeal of the tiny hinge, the chirp of tin on tin, and the soft *whoosh* of a new stack of mail landing on an old stack of mail. Those were the sounds that she tried to ignore—the sounds that ushered in a new day of grief.

"Hungry, Mommy! Hungry now!"

That was a sound that she *couldn't* ignore.

In the kitchen, Ingrid spread peanut butter on toast for her two-year-old son as the telephone jangled in its cradle. "Hello," she whispered. "Yes, this is she. Yes . . . he would have been thirty-one in January. . . . You're welcome."

Ingrid left A.J. to his peanut butter toast and wandered back to the front door. With a bare toe, she pushed aside the catalogs and bills and regarded the dozens of sympathy cards—a literal pile of pity she couldn't bring herself to read. But there, buried in the condolences, Ingrid saw the unmistakable handwriting. *His* handwriting. And a postmark that read September 23, 1973. It was a letter from her husband. A letter from beyond the grave.

* * *

Fort Jackson, South Carolina. September 1966. Ingrid's husband is just another private, waiting in line to make a phone call home. Thanks to what the army called his "issues with authority," this particular private has managed to fail basic training—and that means another six weeks away from his new bride. Ingrid will not be happy.

As he waits his turn to deliver the bad news, the young private does what he always does: he studies the people around him and makes up stories to pass the time.

That guy with the soggy shoes and the hangdog expression, for instance? Maybe he's just come from the carwash pool, where he's been ordered to clean a fleet of muddy jeeps. And the guy with the arm tattoos that read HEY and BABY? Maybe he's a new father. That or a committed ladies' man who wishes to proclaim—in indelible ink—his unshakable belief that women come and go but tattoos are forever.

The private smiles to himself. Ingrid will love that one.

Truth was, Ingrid found all of his stories delightful. But she never thought they would make her rich and never imagined that they would make her a widow. All the same, six years had gone by, and now here she was, her grief temporarily suspended by the shock of seeing a message from the husband she had buried five days earlier. With trembling hands, she opened the envelope, removed

the pages, and began to read her husband's last words: the very words she'd hoped and prayed he would one day say. Moments later, awash in unspeakable grief, Ingrid tried to place a long-distance call to her mother. But when the operator heard Ingrid's last name, she hesitated.

"I hate to ask. Are you any relation?"

Ingrid sobbed. "Yes. He was my husband."

"Oh, honey, I'm so sorry. All the girls down here just loved him. You know that, right? We were his biggest fans."

Ingrid sobbed some more. "I know," she said. "He loved all of you, too."

Back in line, Ingrid's husband turns his attention to the soldier immediately in front of him. The red-rimmed eyes. The hunched-up shoulders. The balled-up fist, gently tapping against his fresh crew cut. He's on the wrong end of a Dear John call, no doubt about it. Ingrid's husband imagines the girl on the other end. A deceitful girl. A girl who has cheated on the soldier with his best friend.

The call ends. The phone slips from the soldier's hand and dangles in midair. Ingrid's husband is close enough to hear the operator say, "Oh, honey, I'm so sorry. Are you still there? Would you like to place another call?"

Blinking back a tear, the soldier grips the receiver and pours his heart out to the operator. Ingrid's husband doesn't eavesdrop. He simply watches the soldier's face and dreams up a little story—just to pass the time.

Eventually Ingrid's husband makes it out of the army and back home. Briefly. He keeps writing stories, but when A.J. arrives and money becomes more of a concern, the former private begins telling his tales to anyone who might pay to hear them. Turns out, Ingrid isn't the only one who likes them. People say they feel so real. They say his characters remind them of their own neighbors.

And so the former private takes his tales on the road, and before long the money begans to roll in. But being away from his family is painful. Ingrid misses her husband, A.J. misses his dad, and the man who used to write stories—just to pass the time—begins to agonize over the days he can never get back. Once, after an all-too-brief visit home, he writes the story of a lonesome troubadour who yearns to relive his favorite days over and over again. People like that one, too. A lot.

Then, just as his career is taking off, Ingrid's husband does the unthinkable: he quits. In his last letter home, the young writer promises to start writing different kinds of stories. Novels and screenplays. Anything that doesn't have to be told night after night, over and over again. He ends his letter with this: "Remember baby, it's the first sixty years that count, and I've got thirty more to go. I love you."

Later that same day, he drops the letter in the mail and boards a private plane that crashes moments after leaving the runway. Five days after that, the postman on Ingrid's porch delivers the best possible news at the worst possible time.

We still remember the characters Ingrid's husband described. The kid in the soggy shoes with a case of the Car Wash Blues. Rapid Roy the Stock Car Boy with one tattoo that said BABY and another one that just said HEY. We still remember the roller derby queen, the pool room hustler no one messed with, the baddest man in the whole damn town, and of course the anonymous telephone operator whose sweet voice calmed a heartbroken soldier at the lowest point of his life.

We remember these characters not only because they feel real, but because the man who brought them to life never made it home. Because his death catapulted his stories to the top of the charts, even as the characters he created ensured his own immortality.

Naturally, Ingrid still has his last letter home. It's kept in a box just for wishes and dreams that will never come true. It is, perhaps, the ultimate love letter—a promise made from beyond the grave by a homesick troubadour who yearned to save time in a bottle. A teller of stories, a singer of songs . . . named Jim Croce.

Late one Tuesday night in the back room at Johnny's, my high school friend Chuck and I listened as old men from the Chorus of the Chesapeake sang the saddest songs ever written. As always, the men were broken down into foursomes, harmonizing around the square tables that held bowls of peanuts and pitchers of draft beer. Things began with "Danny Boy," as they always do, but then moved on to a song I'd never heard before: "Little Pal," an impossibly maudlin tale of a man who must say good-bye to his young son before heading off to prison, for a crime he didn't commit.

Little pal, if Daddy goes away
Promise you'll be good from day to day
Do as Mother says and never sin.
Be the man your daddy might have been . . .

The men stared into each other's faces as they sang and wept unashamedly. "Good Christ!" Chuck said. "That's gotta be the saddest song ever sung!" But Chuck was wrong. As "Little Pal" came to an end, another toe-tapper called "Old Folks" began.

Everyone knows him as Old Folks
Like the seasons, he'll come and he'll go
Just as free as a bird, and as good as his word
That's why everybody loves him so . . .

This song goes on to describe a world where all the old people suddenly drop dead. It's beyond depressing and very powerful. This song actually made me miss my grandparents, which was weird, since they were alive and well at the time.

Once again the men wept as they sang, but before anyone could mourn the death of "Old Folks," another pitch pipe blew and another lamentation began. Are you familiar with a peppy tune called "The Little Boy That Santa Claus Forgot"? No? Neither was I.

> *You know, Christmas comes but once a year for every girl and boy*
> *The laughter and the joy they find in each brand-new toy.*
> *I'll tell you of a little boy that lives across the way*
> *This little fella's Christmas is just another day.*

I'll cut to the chase. The little boy writes to Santa, asking for a soldier and a drum. He's devastated when he gets neither. In fact, the little boy who Santa forgot gets nothing at all for Christmas. Zero. Zilch. Why? Because his father was killed in the war. The "laddie," you see, hasn't got a "daddy."

Chuck stifled a nervous giggle. "Sweet Jesus!" he said. "Who the hell writes a song like that?"

I had no answer to give him, but I did notice that many of the older men who'd been listening were smiling, too—even as they wept. Some actually chortled. Interesting . . . there's nothing funny about orphans and death, shell shock and prison, but when old men sing about pain and loss in four-part harmony, the imagery becomes exponentially more intense. So much so that the songs collapse under the weight of their own mawkishness, leaving you with little choice but to laugh at the unbearable tragedy of it all.

Somewhere across the crowded room, someone blew another pitch pipe and we were treated to the story of an old man living alone for the first time in his life, grieving the loss of his beloved wife. At her grave site, he says:

Dear old girl, the robin sings above you,
Dear old girl, it speaks of how I love you.
The blinding tears are falling, as I think of my lost pearl,
And my broken heart is calling, calling for you
Dear old girl.

The quartet of men who sang that song were all widowers. But there they sat, weeping and smiling and drinking beer and singing into their grief. In the far corner, another pitch pipe blew and the room was treated to a jaunty rumination on crib death. I'm not even kidding. It begins with a father who walks into the nursery, many months after his little girl's death:

I had opened wide the shutters of the long-deserted room
And a flood of golden sunshine chased away the dreary gloom
While gazing 'round with tenderness where baby last had laid
I chanced to see her fingerprints upon the windowpane . . .

How the silent tears were falling
Foolish tears that I wept in vain
But my heart forgot its pains
As I kissed away the stains
Kissed away those fingerprints, off the windowpane.

That was an impossibly depressing tableau—yet even more laughter rang out in the back room at Johnny's as "Fingerprints" came to its weepy conclusion. That's when it occurred to me that those men didn't sing sad songs to reconnect with sadness; they sang them to let sadness go. That's when I understood that those sad old songs took real, heavy feelings and helped distribute their weight. And that brings me to the saddest song I heard on that particular night—a song my old quartet still sings when we get together, every decade or so. A song so sad, Chuck can't get through it without giggling.

Playmates were they, girl and lad,
She's home today, lad feels sad
Doctor who calls, whispers low,
"When the last autumn leaves fall,
Then she must go."

Lad with a tear climbs a tree.
"I'll keep her here," murmurs he.
Big man in blue sternly cries,
"What are you doing there?"
Lad replies,

"I'm tying the leaves so they won't come down;
So the wind won't blow them away,
For the best little girl in the wide, wide world,
Is lying so ill today.
Her young life must go when the last leaves fall;
I'm fixing them fast so they'll stay.
I'm tying the leaves so they won't come down,
So Nellie won't go away."

Can you picture it? A little boy, desperate to keep his playmate from an early grave, tries to prolong her life by tying leaves to a tree! They just don't write 'em like that anymore.

When I learned about Jim Croce's last letter home and the family he left behind, I thought about the little boy up there in the tree, tying the leaves so they wouldn't come down, and I wondered if one day they might sing a song about poor Ingrid, in the back room at Johnny's.

God knows, her story's sad enough.

ONE HELL OF A TOLL

On the day of the great celebration, the invalid looked through his telescope at the crowd gathered below. Thousands of people had already assembled. Hundreds more were on their way, hoping to see the passenger embark upon a most unlikely trip—a trip experts had predicted would never be completed.

The invalid rolled his chair close to the window and considered the price of the little expedition. Fifteen million dollars. Twice as much as what he'd budgeted. Somehow the cost had gotten out of control. Way out of control. Unforgivably, totally, completely out of control. Today we call such profligacy "business as usual." Back then, they called it "the price of progress." Either way, $15 million for a ten-minute trip was one hell of a toll.

Through his telescope, the invalid watched the passenger approach the vehicle, turn to those who had assembled, and begin to speak. He couldn't hear the words, but he knew what was being said. The passenger was thanking the taxpayers for their patience. Thanking them for their faith in the mission. Thanking them for the honor of being the first to go where no man had gone before.

When the passenger finished, the crowd applauded with great enthusiasm. Fireworks exploded. The band began to play. Then, after fourteen years of painstaking preparation, heartbreaking setbacks, and too many obstacles to recall, the passenger climbed into the vehicle, waved to the crowd, and rode off into the history books.

Grimacing in agony with every breath, the invalid watched it all through the lens of his telescope—and wept. Perhaps if his wife had been with him on that historic day, she could have eased his pain. Ever since his escape from that terrible fire, sixty feet below the surface, she'd been trying to treat the mysterious symptoms that continued to plague him. They had begun with the strange tingling in his feet and hands, followed by intense pain in his knees and elbows and inexplicable bruising on his chest and ribs. Then the headaches had begun. Headaches that made him wish he'd stayed below with the men who had perished in that pressurized pit of despair. But his wife had never left his side. Even when the swelling had left him mute. Even when the numbness had left him paralyzed. Even when his skin had begun to molt and slough off in pieces.

Today we call it the bends. Back then, they called it caisson disease. Either way, it was one hell of a toll.

The invalid never recovered, but he did remain on the job, supervising the progress from his bedroom window, always behind his telescope, always racked with pain. His wife became his nurse, his ears, his hands, and his mouth, relaying his instructions to the men who labored below. In her spare time she studied physics, hydrodynamics, and structural engineering. When her husband's condition deteriorated even further, she began to take the meetings that he could no longer attend. Meetings with crooked politicians, ruthless financiers, and a clutch of unscrupulous vendors. Meetings where women were not at all welcome. She attended them anyway. She lobbied hard to prove the experts wrong. And in the end she did.

Through his telescope, the invalid watched the celebration unfold beneath him and continued to ponder the price of progress. Slowly, painfully, he shifted his gaze away from the triumphant passenger and back to the scene of the accident. Not the accident that had left him crippled and ruined but the one that had left him in charge. He found the exact spot on the pier, half a mile away. A slip, a fall, a broken foot, an amputation, an infection, and, just like that, his father—the chief engineer who'd conceived this audacious journey in the first place—was gone.

Of course, it hadn't felt "just like that" at the time. It had taken weeks for the old man to die. First he'd endured mysterious contractions that bent his spine backward, leaving his body arched and twisted. Then he'd contended with spasms that caused his arms to jerk wildly—before they, too, had gone rigid. He'd never forget the way his father's face had slowly retracted from his skull. How the muscles in his head had tightened and seized, pulling the features ever backward. When his father finally died, his eyes were wide and bulging, his teeth bared in a terrible grin.

Today we call it tetanus. Back then, they called it lockjaw.

Either way, it was one hell of a toll.

The invalid lowered his telescope. He brushed away a tear as the passenger slowly rolled off toward the history books. His work was finally done. The trip of a lifetime was now underway. A $15 million excursion that's been repeated so many times since, the original cost has long been forgotten. In fact, in our own century, you can take the same trip for free.

The toll, you see, has already been paid. Paid by the twenty-seven men who were crushed, burned alive, torn in half, and hopelessly mangled in a series of workplace accidents too horrific to describe. Paid by hundreds of other men who lost fingers and toes and other body parts, working on a job site that OSHA would have shut down on day one. Paid by the countless immigrants who labored for two dollars a day in the bottomless pits called "caissons"—pressurized wooden coffins, far below the surface, where forgotten men had dug the foundations by hand and built mighty barbicans one stone at a time. Day after day, week after week, year after year, until limestone towers emerged from the watery depths and scraped the Manhattan sky.

Those were men who'd paid the original toll. Men like John Roebling, the chief engineer and the first man to die during construction. Men like John's son, Washington Roebling, the man who'd inherited his father's title and paid his own heavy price in the caissons—the same man who now watched through a telescope as his wife completed the work that he and his father had started.

Make no mistake, it had been a team effort. A family affair. But Washington's wife was the one who put the ball through the hoop. The self-taught contractor who'd never stopped learning. The unelected official who went toe-to-toe with countless corrupt politicians. The uncredited engineer who won the respect of an army of men—forty years before women were given the right to vote.

Her name was Emily and she, too, understood the price of progress. That was why Emily Roebling was selected to become the first passenger to cross the East River in a horse-drawn carriage on a road experts said could not be built. A road suspended in space, 135 feet above choppy waters. One that had cost over $15 million to create and would not have been there without her extraordinary efforts.

Back then, they called it the eighth wonder of the world. Today we call it the Brooklyn Bridge. Either way, getting it built took . . . one hell of a toll.

The Mighty Mac is a suspension bridge that connects Michigan's Upper and Lower Peninsulas. It's five miles long and 552 feet tall. In May 2007, I painted it. Not all of it; painting the Mackinac Bridge takes a team of maintenance workers seven years to complete. As soon as they're done, they go back to the beginning and start again. Kind of like what I did when I finished the last Travis McGee mystery.

It was windy that day, and as we worked from a scaffold hundreds of feet in midair, covering everything we could reach with a thick layer of "foliage green," I couldn't help but look down and recall the sad fate of Leslie Ann Pluhar. Leslie was crossing the span in September 1989 when a gust of wind blew her Yugo off the deck and sent her plunging into the icy water far below.

Hell of a thing. One minute you're driving across the bridge in your trusty Yugo, cursing the ever-increasing toll. The next, you're free-falling toward oblivion.

Eight years later, the *Dirty Jobs* crew was trying to avoid a similar fate. Along with the hair-raising business of filming hundreds of feet above the water, we shot inside the towers themselves; specifically, inside the small steel compartments that made up the honeycomb-inspired interior. These tiny industrial cubicles needed to be painted with a zinc-based solution that would keep them from rusting. It's hard to choose between the vertigo of working five hundred feet above the water and the claustrophobia of cramming yourself into a coffin-sized steel space with a paintbrush and a respirator. Happily, I didn't have to choose: I got to do both!

Back on the deck, just when I thought we were done, I jokingly suggested to the foreman that we get some footage of me replacing light bulbs on the outer suspension cable. This would have required me to climb over the railing and walk across a steel girder about fifteen feet long, several hundred feet above the water—at around the same place where Leslie Ann's Yugo had gone over the edge. Once across the girder, I would have to step out onto the suspension cable and walk up to the top of the tower, replacing bulbs as I went.

It was a ridiculous suggestion. That was the point: in the history of *Dirty Jobs*, no one had ever allowed me to attempt something so inherently risky. I expected the foreman to laugh along with me. Instead, he said, "Sure! What better way to show your viewers what my guys do every day than let you experience it for yourself?"

Gulp.

Fans of the show will remember that scene. It was one of the most ambitious we ever filmed. We had a helicopter, and it captured every step I took on my long ascent to the top. The footage illustrates the dangers of the work, along with the beauty of the Mighty Mac and the dedication of the men who maintain it day after day. But no one saw the moment, five hundred feet up, when I realized that my safety line wasn't attached.

Suffice it to say, the fault was all mine—a simple lack of concentration.

Here's how it works: As you move up the suspension cable, you have two safety lines that slide up with you, each looped over two smaller cables that function as handrails. Problem is, every ten feet or so, you run into a perpendicular cable between the handrails and the suspension cable. It prevents the safety line from sliding along. You have to unhook each line, one at a time, reattach yourself on the other side, and keep climbing.

After changing dozens of bulbs I'd become increasingly comfortable with this procedure and increasingly confident—overly so. I stopped thinking about what I was doing and began to focus on *how* I was doing, trying to coordinate with the helicopter pilot to get especially good camera angles. As I leaned over to unscrew another bulb, I looked down between my legs at a freighter passing under the bridge. At that height, it looked to be about four inches long, like one of the battleships in the game of the same name. In that moment, I realized I hadn't reattached my safety lines—a realization that nearly caused me to vomit.

Strange, right? Physically, nothing changed when I realized I wasn't secure. I was no less stable than I had been a second earlier. I was at no greater risk of slipping. But the *stakes* of slipping had changed dramatically and, as a result, my sphincter slammed shut and remained that way for the rest of the week. As for the rest of the day, you'd better believe I remained properly tied off and fully focused on the *what* of what I was doing. Screw the how. At five hundred feet in the air, how doesn't matter.

That's the thing about safety nets: their presence impacts everything. Not just when you fall, but when you don't. And this brings me back to the moment I lost my life's savings at the age of thirty-seven. Nothing, really, had changed. Nothing physical, any-way. I still had the skills that allowed me to book as much work as I wanted—no more and no less. I was still healthy, debt free, unencumbered, and able to earn a good living. It's not as if I was Leslie Ann Pluhar, plunging toward oblivion, praying that some-thing or someone would catch me on the way down. But when the feds dragged the trusted financial adviser who'd pretended to be my friend off to prison and explained to me that my safety net was gone, my sphincter slammed shut and stayed that way until I got back on my feet.

But getting back on my feet required me to do something that Travis McGee would have never done: accept a full-time job. I'm referring, of course, to the aforementioned *Evening Magazine*, the inexplicably popular series in San Francisco that afforded me my aforementioned bronze bust, along with a chance to reconstruct my aforementioned safety net, whose sudden disappearance I've just linked to my unplanned walk up the aforementioned Mackinac Bridge—which, I now hope you'll agree, was worth mentioning.

BREAKING THE SILENCE

When Donald Crouch first encountered Jim in his English class in rural Michigan, the aging teacher saw a sullen fourteen-year-old boy. A boy who'd gone deep into a cocoon of self-imposed silence.

Donald might have assumed that Jim was bored or uninterested or even backward. Certainly, he appeared to be all of those things. But there was something in the young boy that lit up whenever the subject turned to poetry. It was subtle, but Donald could see a shift in the boy's posture—a quiet but unmistakable enthusiasm that accompanied any discussion of Chaucer, Shakespeare, or Tennyson.

One day Donald kept Jim after school and tried to get through to the stony-faced boy. Before long, he understood the problem: Jim stuttered. Not a little—a lot. Donald listened patiently as Jim stammered and sputtered and told him about the humiliation he'd lived with for all of his life. Donald understood that Jim had embraced the written word because the spoken word had eluded him.

The next day, Donald told the pupils in his English class to write a poem. The topic didn't matter, as long as it concerned something the pupils were passionate about. That's where fate stepped in, as fate often does—this time in the form of a ruby red grapefruit.

During the Great Depression, rickets and scurvy had become a public health issue in Michigan. The government sent tons of fruit up from Florida to help combat the problem. That very week, a welfare worker had delivered a crateful of grapefruit to Jim's home—and Jim had nearly swallowed his tongue with delight. It was the most incredible, delectable, mouthwatering food he'd ever tasted. That night, Jim wrote his "Ode to a Grapefruit"—a flowery homage to epicurean bliss brought to life by the full, juicy luxury of eating citrus in the dead of a Michigan winter.

Jim turned his poem in the next day, and Donald was stunned by how good it was. Then he did something most teachers would never consider doing today: he put Jim on the spot. Donald had noticed earlier that Jim's stutter vanished whenever he quoted his favorite poets out loud. And so, as he returned the students' assignments with grades and comments attached, Donald addressed the class.

"I've read your poems, and for the most part, I'm pleased," he said. "Some are quite good. Several are excellent. One is . . . extraordinary. Jim, would you kindly come to the front of the class and read us what you've written?"

Jim froze in his seat. The blood rushed to his face. He felt the other students staring at him. Why would his teacher ask him to do such a thing? Jim had trusted Mr. Crouch. Now he felt betrayed.

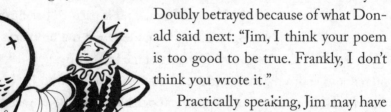

Doubly betrayed because of what Donald said next: "Jim, I think your poem is too good to be true. Frankly, I don't think you wrote it."

Practically speaking, Jim may have been mute, but his hearing was excellent. He couldn't believe his ears. Mr. Crouch was accusing him of *plagiarism?*

"If the words really are yours, Jim, then prove it. Stand and recite them. Right now. Or admit that you stole them."

Jim sprung to his feet and recited "Ode to a Grapefruit" just as he had written it. There was anger in his voice, but what a voice it turned out to be: big and booming and clear as a bell. That was the day Donald Crouch unlocked one of the most powerful and familiar voices in the world. The voice of a boy who stuttered whenever he read aloud, but not when he recited from memory.

As Robert Frost put it, "way leads on to way," and Jim's way was suddenly clear. He became a master of memorization. Reciting poetry led to the debate club. Debate club led to the theater. In time, Jim's newfound vocal prowess took him all the way to Broadway, where he was cast as the lead in Shakespeare's *Othello*—a big part but one that he memorized in no time at all.

A Tony Award followed. Then an Emmy. Then an honorary Oscar. The world, it seemed, was too small to contain a voice as big as Jim's—and so Jim took on the galaxy. A galaxy far, far away . . .

That's how the villainous voice of Darth Vader was created— coaxed from the body of a tremendous performer who might have remained a more silent observer, if not for an extraordinary teacher who understood the power of the spoken word, and the unexpected arrival of a ruby red grapefruit that tasted too good to be true. The unmistakable voice of . . . James Earl Jones.

Like James Earl Jones, I was a painfully shy kid with a deep voice and a weird stammer. My mother still likes to tell stories of how, as a boy, I'd dive under the dining room table when the doorbell rang. Sometimes, according to her, I would vomit at the mere prospect of meeting new people. Happily, the Boy Scouts were on hand to help me out of my shell, along with a teacher no less remarkable than Donald Crouch: my favorite teacher, Fred King.

I was a tall, skinny freshman when we first met, with an encroaching hairline and a larynx the size of a fist. He was "Mr. King," the new music teacher who inherited a choir filled with students like me—students who'd never sung before and thought they were getting a "free period."

From the start, we got much more than we'd bargained for.

Remember George C. Scott's opening speech in *Patton*? Well, Patton was a wimp compared to Fred King. He walked into our classroom that very first day and greeted us with two words that bled into each other: "*Shutup!*"

His voice was stunningly loud. The classroom was instantly quiet. In the silence, he passed out a piece of sheet music far beyond anyone's ability to sight-read. It was a six-part a cappella arrangement in Latin.

There was no way for us to get our bearings—we didn't know how to sight-read—and what's more, there was no time. Mr. King had already blown a pitch pipe, raised his hands, and started to conduct.

I don't know what he was expecting, but the silence that followed seemed to confuse him.

Mr. King looked around curiously. He looked at his hands, as if they were causing the problem. Then he frowned, gave us the pitch one more time, and started conducting again.

Silence.

"This *is* the Overlea High School Concert Choir, is it not?"

Once again silence.

Mr. King closed his eyes. He took several deep breaths, as though trying to calm himself. Then he came unhinged. Smashing one hand on the piano, he launched into a tirade peppered with expressions most often heard in pool halls and saloons. He foamed. He raved. He cursed like the sailor that he had once been as the veins bulged in his neck and forehead. He tore the sheet music to shreds, threw the pieces into the air, and started to rant about "cruel twists of fate," "clueless mutes," and a few other things. Kicking a music stand across the classroom, he bellowed, "If you're not willing to sing, then just *GET THE HELL OUT!*"

A phenomenal exodus followed: half the class bolted and never looked back. I might have joined them, but I had become paralyzed. Who *was* this lunatic? I was still sitting dumbfounded when Mr. King slammed the door shut, popped something into his mouth, and walked back to the piano, glaring at those who had dared to remain. For a long while he stood there, breathing deeply to get himself under control. Then his face cracked in half.

Technically, one might describe what we saw as a "smile." I would describe it as more of a gash—a cruel opening between nose and chin, revealing a rictus of rotten enamel. Tiny teeth—baby teeth—were crowded up against giant incisors. Molars sprouted from spots normally reserved for canines. His front teeth, though properly placed, were the size of small thumbs. They jutted past his ever-widening lips, as if they were trying to escape the diseased gums from which they hung.

Beth Johnson gasped. Cindy Stone screamed. We all recoiled from the dental disaster, and only when we had collected ourselves did Mr. King remove the hideous choppers from his mouth and replace them with human-looking dentures.

"Ladies and gentlemen," he said, "the cowards have all departed. Let's have some fun."

For the next three years, we did. We talked. We laughed. We learned. We marveled at all the false teeth: a grotesque collection designed by a dentist whose sense of humor was no less twisted than Mr. King's own. We learned that our teacher's real teeth had been knocked out years earlier on the gridiron, yet we continued to marvel. You never knew what Mr. King had in his mouth. And you never knew what would come out of it.

With no regard for the standard curriculum—without a shred of political correctness—Mr. King went about the business of spurring, exhorting, and inspiring his students. "Instructing" is too weak a word: He pushed us as no other teacher had dared. He'd give us Vaughan

Williams's *Hodie* and Bach's *Mass in B Minor* to sing—works so far beyond our ability that we didn't know any better than not to try them.

And so we sang those works and many others.

"What, not how!" That's what he'd say. "Always concentrate on *what* you're doing, never how."

It was a valuable lesson. A lesson that I would forget more than once—hell, you just saw me forget it, a couple of pages ago, up on the Mackinac Bridge—but a valuable one, nonetheless.

Anyway, as I was saying, I confessed to Mr. King, early on: "I've never sung before."

In response, he assigned me a solo—one that was several notes out of my range. He kept me after class for private voice lessons, and when he saw that I stuttered, he suggested that I audition for the school play. By "suggested," I mean to say he demanded—and the results were disastrous. Alone on the stage of our school's auditorium, I was stammering my way through a monologue memorized the night before when Mr. King interrupted me.

"Mikey," he said, "I like what you're doing, but this character doesn't stutter, understand? Get into the *character*. *What*, not *how*. You can stutter on your own time."

I didn't think or resist. I didn't argue. I just started over, and this time, I didn't stutter.

A light bulb went on. New possibilities opened before me. I started to act like a nonstuttering person. A more confident person. A person who might, with a little luck, one day explain *How the Universe Works*, or sing arias from Puccini, or sell tchotchkes on live TV, or pickups for Ford, or become marginally famous for gathering sperm from racehorses on prime-time TV. For the moment, I'd settle for the lead in one of our school plays, and a new place in Fred King's mighty Chorus of the Chesapeake. From there I'd play things as they lay and try to remember the virtues of "what, not how."

A simple thing, really, that turned out to be a lot harder than it sounded.

KEEP YOUR VOICE DOWN!

Bob had a voice like a jackhammer, and when he raised it, recruits in the barracks at Eielson Air Force Base awakened as though a shotgun had been fired over their heads.

"Rise and shine, dirtbags! Everybody up! Everybody out! Let's MOVE IT!!!"

As the young men sprang from their bunks, it occurred to Bob that he'd been yelling at recruits for as long as he'd been getting crew cuts. The work of a master sergeant in the air force—Bob's job description—basically came down to yelling.

"Come on, ladies, we're not on vacation. Let's GET THE LEAD OUT!!!"

As the airmen prepared for yet another five-mile run, Bob looked through the frosted windowpanes of the drafty barracks and watched yet another sunrise light up the snowcapped mountains behind Moose Creek, the early-morning rays illuminating the distant clouds . . . the mighty fir trees standing along the riverbank like emerald sentinels . . . the massive boulder in the middle of the rushing

stream where the grizzly bears perched, waiting for the salmon on their way to spawn.

As always, Bob paused to let the image burn itself into his mind's eye. Then he did something rather unusual: he quit. At thirty-eight years of age, the master sergeant vowed right then and there to leave the air force, stop yelling, and get out of the cold. And that is how Bob became a famous TV star.

Actually, it wasn't as easy as all that. It never is. Bob had no experience in front of the camera, and his road to stardom was paved—as such roads often are—with rejection and frustration. But Bob also caught one lucky break—a *very* lucky break—in the form of Annette Kowalski, who first saw him perform in a workshop in Clearwater, Florida. Years later, she recalled their first meeting.

"I was in a deep depression," she said, "grieving the tragic loss of my oldest son. Watching Bob perform changed everything. It wasn't just his talent. It was the way he made me feel. He just lifted my spirits and radiated a quality that I knew America was starving for."

Annette wasn't an agent or a manager, but she knew what talent was when she saw it. So she proposed a business relationship. Bob agreed, and in less than a year, not only did the retired master sergeant have a hit show, he had the number one program on the channel. Eventually he had a body of work that all but eclipsed anyone else's, with four hundred episodes under his belt. And *that* was how Bob became a famous TV star.

Actually, it wasn't as easy as all that. It never is. Annette had no experience managing talent or selling TV shows. She waded through countless "nos" before finding a station manager in Virginia who was willing to put Bob on the air. Once that happened, it really *was* as easy as that—because Annette had been right all along: Bob had a certain quality Americans seemed to be starving for.

Funny thing, though: in an NPR interview in 2016—twenty years after Bob's untimely death at the age of fifty-two—Annette described Bob in a way that shocked listeners. She called him a "tyrant."

"You don't believe that?" she asked. "Do you really think this company would be as successful as it is, if he didn't insist that everything be done a certain way?"

The interviewer was speechless.

"I don't want to leave the impression that he was rude or nasty," Annette added. "He wasn't. But he was very disciplined. Very strict. Believe me, it was Bob's way or no way at all."

NPR's audience might have been surprised by Annette's frank assessment: that wasn't how they'd pictured Bob being at all! But if any of Bob's old recruits had been listening, they wouldn't have batted an eye. Oh, no: "tyrant" would have summed up their former master sergeant nicely. Then again, imagine the shock they had gotten years earlier, when the man with the crew cut who'd screamed at them around the clock had suddenly popped up on their TV screens with an afro the size of a beach ball—and started whispering, in a voice so soft you could call it soporific, about "fluffy little clouds," "happy little trees," and "friendly little boulders to help Mr. Grizzly catch his lunch in our busy little stream."

They would have found it . . . confusing. Yet their sergeant was the very same man Annette Kowalski had discovered in Clearwater, Florida, giving painting lessons to strangers in a hotel conference room. The soft-spoken art teacher who communicated primarily with dashes of titanium white, smidges of cadmium yellow, and touches of Van Dyke brown.

Such was the color palette of the man who pulled Annette Kowalski from the depths of her crippling depression . . . the man who lulled millions of viewers into a hypnotic stupor every week on PBS . . . the master sergeant who'd let his hair grow out and vowed to never again raise his voice.

You might not know him by name, but I bet you've seen *The Joy of Painting*—a little program that lives on forever in reruns, thanks to a man who spent the first part of his life screaming at thousands of recruits in the air force and the rest of it whispering ever so gently to millions of mesmerized viewers. A beloved artist named . . . Bob Ross.

Bob Ross wasn't just an artist, he was a magician—a magician who could turn a blank canvas into a primeval forest or an angry ocean right before our eyes. His secret? There was no secret. Bob Ross worked without a net. He showed us exactly what he was doing and, in the process, gave me and millions of his other viewers the opportunity to follow along, step by step. Odd thing, though: whenever I tried to paint my own "happy little bushes," the results were neither happy nor bushy.

Odd, because the artistic gene runs in my family. My grandmother's sister, Betty, was a terrific painter. So, too, is my cousin, Nancy. She didn't start till she was in her fifties, but once she discovered her talent she never put down the brush. Several of her paintings hang in my home today. To my eye they're every bit as good as anything I've ever seen on *The Joy of Painting*. But, without question, the most skilled artist in my family was an *industrial* artist—my grandfather Carl Knobel.

An electrician by trade, Pop could repair anything. Didn't matter what the "it" was—a broken watch, a faulty furnace, a busted engine—he would either fix it or build a new one from scratch. Pop never made it past the seventh grade, but he was plenty smart. He was also patient, though I never once saw him read the instructions to anything. He just seemed to know how things worked.

When I was still a small boy, my father showed me a bronze plaque in the church we attended; the same church whose basement would become a permanent home for Troop 16. Pop had built much of that church, and that plaque inside it reads:

IN HONOR OF
CARL M. KNOBEL
HUMBLE SERVANT OF JESUS CHRIST
WHO THROUGH THE YEARS HAS GIVEN
HIMSELF TO THE PROGRAM
OF CHRISTIAN EDUCATION AT THE
KENWOOD PRESBYTERIAN CHURCH

"Look at that, son. Your grandfather has a plaque in his honor! Who else do you know with a plaque?"

My grandparents were our next-door neighbors. We had the only two homes at the top of a hill tucked away in a corner of Baltimore County, Mom and Dad and my brothers and me, living no more than a hundred yards away from Nana and Pop. There was room for a cornfield, a pasture where Mom kept her horses, and a big garden up by the woodpile. Off to one side, at the foot of a very steep hill thick with pine trees, you could just hear the traffic flowing off an exit ramp from I-95. My mother told us that the sound was the ocean, and for a while there, we believed her—until a truck hopped the guardrail one day and came halfway up the hill.

Pop built the stable where Mom housed her horses. He'd built the family room in his own home—we gathered there for every holiday; every birthday; every other occasion worth celebrating. In the summer of '75, when my mother started to feel claustrophobic in our modest farmhouse, my grandfather built her a family room, too, along with a patio. His addition to our house was nearly as big as the house itself had been.

Every day that summer, Pop woke up clean and came home dirty. That was his way on any project: he started clean, ended dirty, and somewhere along the way a thing was built or a problem was solved. But *this* project was different. This work was magical, because it unfolded in front of my wondering eyes. Where there had been grass, there was suddenly a foundation. Where there had been empty air, there were now walls and a roof. Then there were windows and a fireplace—and then, in a twinkling, the summer was over and Mom had a family room of her own.

I studied Pop's every move on the construction site, determined to follow in his footsteps. I became his apprentice that summer and loved it. Odd thing, though: none of the work we were doing made sense to me, and things were no easier in school. In woodshop, I made a sconce that looked more like an amoeba. Pop nodded when I showed it to him and applauded my "creative" design. In metal shop, I made a steel safe that didn't quite close. (I had also put the hinges on the wrong side.) I got an F, and this time I asked Pop if he thought the "handy gene" might be recessive. He laughed.

"There's nothing magical about what I do, Mike. I'm just using the tools I was given. You can be a tradesman, too, if that's what you want to be. Heck, we're *all* tradesmen. The trick is to get the right toolbox."

Was that the best advice Pop ever gave me? That's hard to say. But without question, it was the best advice I ever took.

THE BIGGEST NAME IN TOWN

High in the hills of a town without pity, a stubborn sun slowly set on a warm September evening, even as a young starlet walked up the shoulder of some canyon road and out onto the property of the biggest name in town. She was apprehensive, understandably so. Partly because it was getting dark . . . partly because she was trespassing . . . partly because she was about to murder someone.

For the record, the starlet was not violent by nature. But desperate times called for desperate measures. The studio head, a big man in town, was also a feckless fool without taste or common sense. He had all but cut her out of the film that would have made her famous. Just like that, in the blink of an eye, her long-anticipated debut on the silver screen had been reduced to a pile of celluloid on the cutting room floor.

Could she have called HR? Could she have lodged a formal complaint with the studio? No. This betrayal would not be remedied with a hashtag and a me-too. This was personal. The starlet steeled herself for the task at hand, double-checked the contents of her purse, and approached the sprawling property of the biggest name in town.

Five stories above her, the legendary icon looked down as the starlet approached. Her appearance was not exactly a surprise. Beautiful girls often came to this very spot. Usually they came around sunset. This girl, however, was a real looker. She was twenty-four, flaxen hair, alabaster skin, eyes that were bluer than a Montana sky. Oh yes, girls like her were always welcome here. Pretty young things with stars in their eyes, happy to barter everything they had for the one thing they didn't.

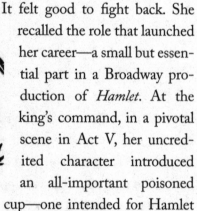

Five stories below, the starlet was smiling—smiling, in spite of her dark purpose. It felt good to fight back. She recalled the role that launched her career—a small but essential part in a Broadway production of *Hamlet*. At the king's command, in a pivotal scene in Act V, her uncredited character introduced an all-important poisoned cup—one intended for Hamlet but consumed accidentally by the king's wife and Hamlet's mother, Gertrude. The starlet recalled that performance so clearly. It was more than worthy of an encore, of that she was sure.

But enough with the memories: back to the task at hand. She knew the way in. She knew that her target was on the top floor. In her mind's eye, she saw herself ascending each step carefully, one at a time. Up at the top, the view was sure to be breathtaking. The sun was now beneath the horizon. The lights of Tinseltown would be twinkling all the way out to the Pacific. But she would not be distracted. The role she was playing tonight was that of a cold-blooded killer—and she would play it to the best of her ability. She would betray nothing of her true intentions. She would simply wait till the moment was right—and then she would show the biggest name in town what *real* power looked like.

The starlet checked the contents of her purse one last time. She made sure that everything was exactly where it should be. Then she began her careful climb up to the fifth story, where she delivered a truly Oscar-worthy performance.

A hiker found the corpse three days later. A mangled body in a nearby ravine.

Detectives were called, but you didn't have to be a hard-boiled gumshoe or a Sunset Boulevard shamus to figure out who done it. The cops knew all about the starlet's abrupt removal from *Thirteen Women*—her first and last major motion picture. They knew all about the financial difficulties that followed, along with the nude photographs for which she had been paid to pose. But it was the contents of her purse that closed the case just moments after it had been opened—specifically, a short note that read, "I am afraid I am a coward. I am sorry for everything. If I had done this a long time ago, it would have saved a lot of pain."

And that's how the curtain fell on the final act of Peg Entwistle, a gifted actress who left a promising career on the stage to try her luck in Los Angeles. Alas, the only performance for which she's remembered today is the one she delivered on that warm September evening back in 1932, at a famous address on the rocky slopes of Mount Lee, high in the hills of the town without pity. It was there, at the end of a canyon road called Beachwood, that poor Peg—her spirit broken by empty promises and shattered dreams—made good on her promise to kill someone by climbing the rungs of a rickety ladder, scrambling onto the top of a giant "H," and throwing herself off the Hollywood sign.

It was, after all . . . the biggest name in town.

You want to hear a host story?

I don't blame you. As the host of cultural touchstones like *Worst-Case Scenario* and *How Booze Built America*, I'm partial to them myself. But my favorite host story is the one I experienced firsthand at a production company in Burbank, back in 1997.

Like Peg Entwistle's tale, mine is full of hope and ambition. It, too, involves one of the biggest names in town. Unlike Peg's story, mine has a happy ending, thanks to an excellent piece of advice that I still try to follow whenever I'm in front of a camera. I want to share that advice with you, because writing about Peg made me wonder where I'd be without the many words of wisdom I've received over the years. Maybe, if someone had pulled Peg aside at just the right time and said just the right thing, she would have gone on to her own, long career. Maybe she'd have a star on Hollywood's Walk of Fame. Maybe she'd have written her own book about it.

We'll never know, sadly. But what I *do* know is that, way back in 1997, a producer named Tom Frank was looking for a game show host, and my tape must have made an impression.

"This is the worst demo tape I've ever seen," he said. "There's nothing on there but mistakes and outtakes."

"Thanks," I said. "I try to manage expectations."

"Mission accomplished," he said. "It made me wonder if you were stable."

"You'll have to hire me to find out," I said.

"Would you like to hear about the project first?"

"Please," I said. "The anticipation is killing me."

Tom Frank talked fast, sounding like all producers do when they explain an idea they've explained a thousand times to a thousand people they'll never talk to again. "The show's called *No Relation*. The fX Channel has just bought forty episodes."

"What's The fX Channel?" I asked. "Did FOX lose a vowel?"

Tom Frank ignored the question. "The show works like this:

On each episode, a celebrity panel attempts to determine which member of a family of five is not related to the other four. In round one, celebrities question the contestants individually. In round two, they question the family together and compare their notes. They make their best guess. Then the impostor reveals him or herself and brings out the actual family member that they've been impersonating."

"Are there fabulous prizes?"

"Depends on how many celebrities are fooled. If none of them guess correctly, the impostor gets a thousand bucks and the family gets an all-expenses-paid trip to Mexico. What do you think?"

"To tell you the truth," I said, "it sounds like *To Tell the Truth*."

"Yeah, well . . . there's no such thing as a new idea. But this is a very big deal for the network."

It sounded like a guaranteed failure, which was precisely what I was looking for. It's what I always looked for in those days: a few months of steady work, followed by a quick cancellation, followed by a few months of premature retirement. Perfect. Travis McGee 101.

"I'm your man," I said. "When do I start?"

"I'm not offering you the job," Tom Frank said. "I'm offering you an audition. Tomorrow morning at 9:00 a.m."

"Great. What do game show hosts wear nowadays?"

"Wear a sport coat. Slacks. Button-down shirt. No tie."

"Wouldn't it be easier if you just gave me the job now?" I asked.

"Honestly, I'm not even sure I should give you the address."

He did, though, and I arrived ten minutes early the next morning at an office building in Burbank. A pretty receptionist handed me a script and led me to a conference room where a dozen other guys were pacing around, memorizing the same words, muttering to themselves in the same practiced baritones. Button-down shirts, slacks, and sport coats. No ties. We looked like mannequins recently escaped from the same haberdashery.

One guy in particular was a composite of every game show host I'd ever seen. He had white teeth and a suspicious tan and seemed so supremely confident that I wondered if he had already gotten the gig. He reminded me of a very young Dick Clark—who was, for my money, the best game show host ever. I loved the way Clark leaned against the podium while explaining the rules on *The $25,000 Pyramid*. Not a care in the world. As the stakes increased, he didn't get ramped up—he got more laid back. Dick Clark hosted like Perry Como sang: warm, genuine, with a touch of insouciance. How would Dick Clark have handled *No Relation*?

I was the last to be called. On a mock stage, three "celebrities" sat on a sofa. Their name tags read "Tom Hanks," "Julia Roberts," "Shelley Long." Five production assistants, who also had name tags, were sitting in folding chairs across from them. They were "The Johnsons." At the far end of the room, there was a video camera, a large monitor, and a partition. Behind the camera, in front of the partition, a small group of people huddled and conferred: the suits. Tom Frank was among them.

We bantered for a moment. Then Frank said "Action!," and I immediately went off script, channeling my inner Dick Clark.

"Hello, everyone, and welcome to *No Relation*. It's nice to see you all again. I'm Mike Rowe, and these are the Johnsons. Well, at least four of them are. One of them is actually an impostor who has assumed the identity of the missing Johnson, who is bound and gagged in the trunk of my car. I'm kidding! The missing Johnson is backstage and will remain there as our celebrity judges question the real Johnsons and try to find out which one of them is . . . No Relation! Before we begin, let's meet our celebrity judges."

We pretended to play for twenty minutes or so. At first, I was put off by the fact that Tom Hanks had a Mohawk and Julia Roberts looked like my grandmother. The Johnson family was also confusing: the parents were white, the daughter was Asian, the son was black, and the grandmother appeared to be Hispanic—a configuration that added new layers of complexity to the show's central question but spoke well of the production company's commitment to diversity in the workplace. Nevertheless, I worked through, guiding the conversation, making mild, mostly tasteful jokes, and trying not to look too hard at "Shelley Long"—who looked and sounded just like Shelley Long, which I found to be doubly distracting. We were rolling along pretty well when Tom Frank said "Cut!" and walked toward me.

"Tell me," he said. "Is that your lucky jacket?"

"Don't know yet," I said. "I borrowed it from a friend."

The coat I was wearing belonged to my high school friend Chuck, on whose couch I'd been crashing in Hollywood. It was electric blue with a slight bias toward periwinkle.

"Does your friend work for the circus?"

"Worse," I said. "He sings barbershop." At which point a really weird thing happened. A shocking thing. Dick Clark stepped out from behind a partition and said, "Hello."

Every so often, the universe behaves in ways that leave me mute. This was one such occasion. Had I just conjured Dick Clark out of thin air? Was I seeing some sort of phantom? A ghost? It sure felt that way. One minute, I had been channeling Dick Clark. Now he was here, and I couldn't quite square it.

"That was great! Really nice work."

I was speechless. Gobsmacked. Flabbergasted.

"By the way," the ghost said, "I'm Dick Clark."

"That is correct!" I replied, as if I were hosting a game show.

It really was him.

Dick Clark laughed in a completely warm, genuine way. "Welcome to my production company. Thanks for coming by! You're a natural. I've seen some of your work. But tell me, have you hosted a game show before?"

"No, I haven't. But I've done a lot of live television." I was hoping he didn't know that I had been thrown out of the home shopping industry.

"Tom tells me you were thrown out of the home shopping industry," Dick Clark said. "What happened?"

I cleared my throat and glanced at Tom, who was clearly enjoying the moment. "There was a mutual consensus that my skills were . . . inconsistent with the expectations of that particular genre."

Dick Clark laughed again. "I bet you have some great stories!"

"One or two," I said as another suit stepped out from behind the partition. "Mike, this is Rich Ross. He calls the shots over at fX."

Rich Ross looked a lot younger than I would have expected.

"Hi, Mike," he said. "We're big fans over at the network. We'd love to see you again."

Dick Clark nodded in agreement.

"Can you come back in a few days?" Ross asked.

"Sure," I said.

Then Dick Clark stepped closer to me and lowered his voice. "Can I give you some advice?" he asked.

I thought he was going to comment on Chuck's jacket. That, or tell me to stick to the script. But he didn't. Instead he imparted a secret—a treasured bit of advice that was so obvious and so good I was certain the moment I heard it, I'd never forget it.

I was wrong about that, of course. But it's nice to feel certain every now and again. . . .

CHARLIE'S BIG BREAK

Charlie knew he had a hit the moment he picked up the guitar. The tune seemed to write itself. The words tumbled out of his mouth as though he had known them all his life. Like every other aspiring musician who had come to Los Angeles with stars in his eyes, Charlie needed a break—a chance to show everyone just who he was and what he was capable of.

Now, finally, that chance had come.

Seated across from him were two major players in the music biz: the Legendary Drummer, who'd befriended him a few weeks earlier, and the Legendary Producer—a man credited with shaping the "California Sound." Either man could have made Charlie famous—literally overnight.

Charlie stroked the neck of his acoustic guitar, took a deep breath, and began to play. And really, it could not have gone better. The Legendary Producer nodded in time with the music. The Legendary Drummer hummed along in harmony. It was the kind of audition every performer dreams of giving, and when the song came to an end, Charlie knew he was a few steps closer to stardom. The

Legendary Drummer said, "Hell, yeah!" The Legendary Producer said, "Damn. Let's make an album."

And so they did.

Over the next few weeks, Charlie recorded four original songs. With the help of the Legendary Drummer and two of his Legendary Bandmates, Charlie found the magic every famous musician tries to capture in the studio. But the Legendary Producer had issues with some of the lyrics. He wanted something "softer." Something more "relatable."

Like any true artist, Charlie was not inclined to compromise his work. He pushed back. He had something important to say, damn it, and no producer, however legendary, was going to boss him around. Really, who did the guy think he was? These were *Charlie's* songs, and Charlie would sing them the way he wanted!

Long story short, Charlie blew it. He alienated the very people he needed most. The Legendary Producer stopped taking his calls. The Legendary Drummer went back to being a rock star.

Charlie took it hard and, by all accounts, handled the rejection quite badly. One day, after weeks of being ignored, he confronted the Legendary Drummer at his home on Sunset Boulevard. He'd brought a gift along: a single bullet.

"What's this for?" the Legendary Drummer asked.

"It's for you," said Charlie. "Every time you look at it, I want you to think how nice it is that your kids are still safe."

That did it. The Legendary Drummer was not one to take a threat lightly—especially one directed toward his family. Charlie should have known that. And so the Legendary Drummer beat Charlie—beat him like the drums he pummeled for a living. Then he threw Charlie to the floor and beat him some more. He beat Charlie until Charlie wept like a baby. But the hardest blow had yet to fall.

One year later, a broke, unemployed Charlie was killing time in a record shop. There he saw a poster of the Legendary Drummer, playing onstage with his Legendary Brothers. They had a new single out, "Bluebirds over the Mountains," a cover of an old rockabilly song.

"Jesus," said Charlie, "what a bunch of hacks. They don't even write their own songs anymore."

The B-side, however, was an original: "Never Learn Not to Love," it was called. Charlie was curious, naturally. He shoplifted the record, and later that night—seconds after dropping the needle on the vinyl—he dropped his beer on the floor and collapsed onto the sofa in a stupefied rage. They had changed the title. They had altered a few of the lyrics. But the rest was identical! It was the same song that he had auditioned with—only now it was being sung by the Legendary Drummer: Dennis Wilson.

No one can say if having his song stolen by the Beach Boys

pushed Charlie over the edge. But no one can deny that in the months that followed, Charlie paid a visit to the home of that Legendary Producer—a man named Terry Melcher. Melcher then moved to Malibu, which was good news for him but not so good for the new residents of his old home. Those people were all murdered in the most brutal fashion imaginable. Thus began a killing spree that led to the trial of the century and eventually brought Charlie the fame that he had so desperately sought.

For whatever it's worth, Charlie's audition song had originally been called "Cease to Exist"—which Charlie stubbornly refused to do. Long after his Legendary Drummer and his Legendary Producer had shuffled off their mortal coils, Charlie sat rotting in his jail cell, waiting for the big break that never seemed to come—until it finally did, forty-six years later. A *really* big break that finally rid the world of a mass murderer named . . . Charles Manson.

"Never Learn Not to Love." See what the Beach Boys did there? With the judicious deployment of a single double negative, Manson's "Cease to Exist" suddenly sounds a lot less deranged and much more like a Zen koan. That's how Dick Clark's advice had struck me, back when I was auditioning to host *No Relation*:

"Next time, don't say hello to *everyone*."

I was confounded: What did *that* mean? My expression conveyed my confusion.

"When you looked into the lens," he said, "your first words were 'Hello, *everyone*.' That's probably not the best way to say hello."

"It's not?"

"No. And when you said, 'It's nice to see you all again,' that's also a mistake."

"It is?"

"Yes. People don't see themselves as part of a crowd, Mike. They see themselves as *individuals*. They want a personal connection with someone they can trust. Your job is to be that person. That's what a good host does. He becomes a guest in the viewer's home."

I realized just then that I was still shaking Dick Clark's hand, even though he had stopped shaking mine. I let his go, and he put it on my shoulder.

"When you talk to the camera, Mike, don't think about every-body. Think about one person. Someone you know. Someone you like. Talk to *them*. And if you say, 'It's nice to see you again,' make damn sure you *mean* it."

"Thanks, Mr. Clark. I'll do that."

"You can call me Dick," he said. "All my friends do."

The next day, Tom Frank called me back—it had come down to me and that one other guy—the young kid with the white teeth and the suspicious tan.

Maybe it was Chuck's lucky blue jacket. Maybe they flipped a coin. I don't know, but in the end I was chosen to host *No Relation*. We shot forty episodes that summer, on the same stage as *The Price Is Right*. I shared a dressing room with Bob Barker. (Not at the same time, naturally.) We might have shot another season, but *No Relation* was canceled, just as I had predicted. Thanks to a revolving door of dim-witted celebrities who lacked the where-withal to root out impostors, I wound up giving away our entire allotment of grand prizes before the first ten episodes had even aired. Tom Frank was beside himself. To this day, he refers to the show as *Hola, Acapulco!*, which was where all our contestants ended up going.

I sometimes wonder if *No Relation* would have been a hit if Dick Clark had hosted as well as produced it. I bet he could have steered those dim-witted celebrities in the right direction. He was, after all, a master broadcaster. A host who was really a guest. A guest who'd come to me as a ghost. A ghost on my television who always seemed happy to see me—even though I knew he could not.

As for Tom Frank—he might not be the biggest name in town, but he's done okay. So, too, has the kid with the white teeth and the suspicious tan—a kid named Ryan who missed out on *No Relation* and wound up saddled with a steady gig he can't seem to escape, on a show called *American Idol*.

BOBBY BRINGS
HOME THE BACON

At the Grammy Awards, Britney Spears forgot to thank the pig. No one called her on it, but looking back, the facts are clear: without that pig, Britney would have never sold a hundred million albums. No way. Likewise, Steven Spielberg would have never gotten *Jurassic Park* to the big screen, and Neil Armstrong would never have walked on the moon. Yet none of these people ever acknowledged the pig. Bobby, on the other hand? He thought about that pig every day. Why wouldn't he? Thanks to the pig, Bobby died with a net worth of $3.2 billion and a product that had changed . . . everything.

Fundamentally, Bobby was a tinkerer and risk taker. But not necessarily in that order. When he was twelve, he built a box kite, strapped it to his back, and dove off the roof of Grinnell College in Iowa—just to see if he could fly. Turned out he could. For about thirty seconds.

There was also the time he took a propeller, welded it to the back of his sled, and hooked it up to an engine from an old washing machine. Turned out, motorized sleds don't fly, either. But they do go faster than normal sleds. Much faster.

Bobby was a tinkerer, you see. A risk taker. But not necessarily in that order. And not just as a boy. When he was twenty-one, he volunteered to procure the guest of honor for a fraternity luau. Under the light of a harvest moon, low and fat in the Iowa sky, the young physics major regarded his options, grunting and rooting around in the muddy pigpen. There were so many to choose from. The farmer wouldn't miss just one swine . . . would he?

Not twelve hours later, the guest of honor was turning slowly over an open fire, roasting to a crispy golden brown with an apple wedged in its mouth. By all accounts, it was a very successful luau— but the next day, a moral hangover weighed heavily upon Bobby. What had he been thinking? The pig had not been his to take—yet he had taken it. As the son of a preacher, he should have known better. And so Bobby returned to the burgled pigpen, confessed his crime to the farmer, and offered to compensate him.

If the farmer had let bygones be bygones, who knows what our world would look like today? But of course the farmer didn't, because stealing a pig in Iowa back in 1948 was like rustling cattle in Colorado a hundred years earlier. It was larceny—especially in Grinnell, where any physics major could have told you that every action had an equal and opposite reaction. Like the good Christian he was, the farmer forgave Bobby's sin. But he still had to press charges. Even though the sheriff liked Bobby, he still had to arrest him. Even though the dean of the college admired Bobby, he still had to expel him. As for the preacher, who loved his son, well, there was nothing he could say in the face of such obvious guilt—and so, he said nothing.

But not everyone believed that the reaction to Bobby's crime had been equal or opposite or even just.

Grant Gale, a physics professor at Grinnell College, came to Bobby's defense. He implored the dean, the sheriff, the mayor, and all the good people in town to rethink the penalty for purloined pork and find a punishment that fit the crime.

In the end the farmer dropped the charges, the sheriff backed off, and Bobby's expulsion was reduced to a one-semester suspension.

For some students, that might have translated into a four-month vacation, but not for Bobby. Because in the midst of Grinnell's Great Swine Scandal, Professor Gale had received a very interesting package in the mail—a package that contained two prototypes from Bell Laboratories sent to him by a Grinnell graduate.

The professor was intrigued. He used one of the prototypes to demonstrate the flow of electrons through a solid in what turned out to be the very first college class ever offered in solid-state electronics. And the other prototype? That wound up in the hands of the suspended senior who liked to tinker and take risks. But not necessarily in that order.

You see, if Bobby hadn't spent endless hours tinkering with that prototype—the first transistor produced by Bell Labs—there would have been no small step for Neil Armstrong, because Apollo 11 would not have had an on-board computer. For Steven Spielberg, there would have been no *Jurassic Park*—because there would have been no computer-generated imagery. And for Britney Spears, there would have been no Grammy Awards—because there would have been no Auto-Tune.

The exact details of how Bobby transformed the modern age would fill a book—a book best written by a physicist, or someone who *really* understands how the universe works. But this much can be explained by me: without Bobby's willingness to assume risks, all of his tinkering would have been for naught—because if you think diving off a roof strapped to a homemade kite is risky, try launching a start-up in Silicon Valley before the silicon's even there.

That's exactly what Bobby did, back in 1968. And even though you might not know his name, you know what's inside: inside your coffee machine, your electric razor, your car, your remote control, your kids' favorite toy, your Fitbit, your laptop, and of course the smartphone you can't leave home without. It's the very same thing that Bobby was tinkering with during his fortuitous suspension from college. The same thing they're still tinkering with today at a company called Intel.

That's the legacy of Robert Noyce—a man who liked to tinker and take risks, but not necessarily in that order. But let's not forget Bob's silent partner: a twenty-five-pound suckling pig whose impact on our lives began with a brief appearance at a long-forgotten luau in America's heartland. A pig whose sacrifice gave us a tiny piece of silicon we call . . . the microchip.

Forty years after Robert Noyce put a pig on a spit and transformed the world—one year before I put a pig on a pedestal and transformed my blue jeans—another Robert was doing things with pigs that could not be ignored. And so, they weren't. This Robert became the most popular character we ever featured on *Dirty Jobs*. And those pigs of his? They finished the job that legions of tourists and gamblers could not.

For fifty years, Bob Combs drove his ancient pickup truck up and down the Las Vegas strip, loaded it up with uneaten buffet food from high-end hotels and casinos, and returned to his modest farm in north Las Vegas. There, in an otherwise normal backyard, he shoveled the spoils into a massive cooker, a towering, Rube Goldbergian contrivance that transported the smorgasbord into a giant stewpot located three stories above the ground. It wasn't high tech, but it worked. Before long, the grub was reduced to a viscous, beigey bouillabaisse.

Bob told my field producer, Barsky, that the smell reminded him of a bakery.

He'd built the entire contraption himself with parts cobbled together from local junkyards. And so, tons of uneaten people food—waste that would have wound up in the landfill—ended up filling the troughs on his farm. Thanks to Bob, a city that traffics in excess suddenly had a conservation program worth bragging about.

I accompanied Bob as he drove that ancient pickup down from the cooker to the troughs, with boiling slop sloshing over the roof, down the windshield, and onto the hood. Barsky's eyes widened as hundreds of ravenous pigs descended upon the leftovers. I can still hear the crescendo of squealing and slurping that accompanied this wild and gluttonous scene. It was epic. Just . . . epic.

To this day, people ask me about Bob Combs. I tell them that he was a cross between Jimmy Stewart and Old MacDonald—the living embodiment of everything *Dirty Jobs* had set out to highlight: a modest, good-humored man, armed with an extraordinary work ethic; a man who had found a new angle and thrived in a business with very tight margins. As grain prices rose, squeezing all of the farmers around him, Bob kept drawing from his endless supply of leftovers. It was hard work, to be sure, but it was good for his business, good for the environment, and very good for the city of Las Vegas. But when we first met, in 2006, Bob was a man besieged by an army of angry acronyms—HSUS, EPA, OSHA—as well as his neighbors, who wanted to close his operation down because his pig farm smelled like . . . a pig farm.

Las Vegas was booming, and a pig farm wasn't what hundreds of homeowners wanted so close to their brand-new homes. They didn't care that Bob had been there for decades. They didn't care that Bob was providing a valuable public service. The only thing they cared about was the smell—and making it go away.

Developers fumed. Committees formed. Petitions were circulated, and hearings were held. The pressure to close down Bob's farm was unrelenting, but Bob held fast and I'm glad he did, because after that *Dirty Jobs* episode aired, the developers tried a different tack:

they pooled their resources and offered to buy Bob's property. They offered him a staggering sum: 75 million dollars.

Bob passed.

"Bob," I said. "What are you thinking? It's 75 million dollars."

Bob replied, "Yeah. But what would I do with my pigs?"

"I don't know," I said. "Kill them? Eat them? You're going to anyway, right?"

Bob didn't have anything to say to that. But it occurred to me later that his real question wasn't "What would I do with my pigs?" It was "What would I do without them?"

Bob Combs had put his pigs on a pedestal years before I came along. He knew what mattered most to him. It was the work, you see. Work that would have ceased had he taken the money. Work that defined him, even though he was approaching his eightieth year. Work that he was simply not ready to abandon.

"I kinda like the smell," he told me. "I guess I've gotten used to it."

THE GREASEMAN COMETH

The grease man dragged his shovel across the wooden floor and stabbed it into the towering pile of coal with a satisfying crunch.

Technically, this was a job for the fireman—but the grease man wasn't one to complain. In 1869, complaining on the Michigan Central Railroad got you nowhere. Lifting with his legs and pivoting with his hips, the grease man flipped his wrist, sent the anthracite sailing through the air, and watched it vanish into the furnace's gaping mouth. The sounds of his work kept time with the tempo of the train that swayed beneath him—a steady Sisyphean rhythm propelling man and machine through America's heartland.

As the grease man shoveled, it occurred to him that his body worked a lot like the engine he fed: the more fuel he gave it, the faster it went. But when the train slowed and ground to a sudden halt—for the fifth time that day—the grease man stopped thinking in metaphors and prepared himself for the job at hand: the job that no one wanted but somebody had to do. Armed with an oil can, a giant brush, and a bucket of rendered animal fat, he jumped from the engine car and began the business of lubricating the axles, as well as every piece of exposed metal inside the locomotive's engine. It was tough work, it was hot work, but there was no getting around it.

Back then, locomotives were constantly shutting down for oiling and loosening. So, too, were engines and wheels and machines in factories all over the world. Everything that moved needed lubrication, and nothing could be lubricated while it was moving. Thus the wheels of civilization could only turn as quickly as the grease man could work. And so, after ten minutes of contortions underneath several boxcars and inside the engine itself, our hero emerged looking very much like a glazed doughnut. Sweat streamed down his forehead and stung his eyes. Chunks of animal fat clung to his overalls and skin. Was he resentful? Did he believe that his fancy apprenticeship at a prestigious machine shop in Scotland entitled him to something more than a job shoveling coal and slathering lubricant into the entrails of this iron horse? The short answer is "no." But the grease man didn't think about that. He was too thirsty to think—very, very thirsty. Yet as he gulped down cup after cup of cool water, he was struck once again by the similarities between a hardworking engine and a hardworking railroad man. Along with copious amounts of fuel, both required plenty of internal lubrication.

The grease man refilled his empty cup and wondered aloud, "What if a train could be hydrated as easily as a man?"

It was a good question, and for the next year he tinkered in his workshop, determined to find an answer. Eventually he perfected a prototype and applied for a patent. His device was simple: a reservoir of oil that used gravity to deliver just enough of the lubricant to wherever it was needed while the engine was still running. He called it a lubricating cup. If it worked, locomotive engines would no longer need to stop in order to be oiled. True, a mechanical solution would eliminate his own job. But, all things considered, it seemed like a risk worth taking.

As it turned out, the lubricating cup *did* work—and the impact on productivity and mobility was astounding. Word of this breakthrough spread all over the country; soon every engineer and conductor from Tacoma to Tallahassee was demanding one.

Obviously, the grease man was in no position to leap into mass production. So, for the next few years, cheap imitations popped up everywhere. They all promised the same results, but none proved as reliable as the original. In fact, most of the knockoffs made the problem even worse. If it wasn't the grease man's original lubricating cup, it just wasn't worth the price.

Over the next sixty years, the grease man would apply for and receive fifty-six additional mechanical patents. His work revolutionized the Industrial Revolution. He invented the ironing board along the way (his wife was tired of steaming his shirts), as well as the sprinkler (he was tired of watering his lawn). But it was the lubricating cup he came up with that changed the pace of modern civilization and helped build the infrastructure we rely upon today.

According to Thomas Edison, "Genius is one percent inspiration and ninety-nine percent perspiration." If he had consulted with the grease man, whose name was Elijah, he might have assigned a few percentage points to lubrication—and emancipation, as well. Because long before Elijah was greasing wheels on the Michigan Central Railroad, hundreds of anonymous men and women were quietly greasing different sets of wheels on a different set of tracks: tracks that carried Elijah's parents from a plantation in Kentucky to a small town in Canada. There, the grease man had been born—unlike his father, a free man.

Thanks to the Underground Railroad, Elijah was afforded an opportunity. Thanks to his parents, Elijah was afforded an apprenticeship. And thanks to his work ethic and his unquenchable thirst to build a better mousetrap, Elijah was afforded so much success that his last name still resonates today. You know it. You've probably used it. It's a slave name that's become synonymous with everything authentic, everything original—a name we invoke today whenever our search for the genuine article leads us to ask . . . "Is that the real McCoy?"

"You can't script the Bering Sea."

Phil Harris said that at another one of our roundtable *After the Catch* conversations. We were having a round of duck farts and discussing the strange appeal of *Deadliest Catch* when Phil offered that brilliant rejoinder. He repeated it under his breath seconds later as he lit one more cigarette.

"You can't script the Bering Sea."

"Damn," I said. "Why do you say the best stuff when the cameras aren't rolling?"

Phil shrugged. "Why do you ask the best questions during commercials?"

I laughed and repeated the same question a few minutes later. But of course, with the cameras rolling, Phil gave a different answer—as I knew he would.

"It's the narrator," he said. "He's the secret to our success. That sexy devil could make anything sound exciting."

"Well," I said, "there's no accounting for taste."

The captains laughed and we moved on to another topic, but I had been struck once again by Phil's stubborn refusal to repeat himself. He saw second takes as a performance. It drove the producers crazy, because Phil said so many great things off camera. But Phil figured reality TV ought to be real, and he did his best to keep it that way.

"What the hell happened?" he asked during the next break. "One minute, I'm watching Jacques Cousteau, Jane Goodall, and David Attenborough. Now all I see are 'real' housewives who ain't real at all and 'survival' experts drinking their own pee. What the hell's next?"

He threw another duck fart back and lit one more cigarette.

"You're right," I said. Because he was. Not long after that conversation, the Amish got a Mafia, the Ducks got a Dynasty, Honey got a Boo-Boo, and "reality" TV became profoundly unreal. Today it's about making moonshine, flipping houses, panning for gold, pawning crap in storage lockers, and getting yelled at by angry chefs who've been paid to get angry. Everyone else is *Naked and Afraid*.

I've seen the scripts for many of those "unscripted" shows. Believe me, they exist—and they're no less detailed than the script of a sitcom or a movie. But one thing's for sure: no matter how hard Hollywood tries to "produce" reality, Phil got it right. You can't script the Bering Sea.

There was a great moment in Anthony Bourdain's show *Parts Unknown*. Phil Harris didn't live to see it, but he would have loved it. Tony goes scuba diving for octopi in Sicily—but there are no octopi to be found. Then, out of nowhere, they appear—all around him. Unbeknown to Bourdain, a local producer is dropping them off the side of the boat above him.

Imagine the scene: Bourdain is twenty feet down with his cameraman and his spear when store-bought frozen octopi begin to float by his head. That's what any "reality" producer in my business would do to "salvage" a scene—but it makes Bourdain crazy. He's so appalled, he does the only sensible thing he can think to do: he starts drinking in protest and continues to drink for the rest of the episode, to the point where he's useless on camera. Later on, in voice-over, he rips into the producer for attempting to fool his viewers and demands that CNN air the raw footage. Which, to its credit, CNN does. The one time I got to meet Tony, I complimented him on that episode. Like Joan Rivers, Phil Harris, and the Bering Sea, Tony couldn't be scripted.

On the very first season of *Deadliest Catch*, back before anyone understood what the show might become, someone at the network thought crab fishing would make for a terrific game show. I'm not kidding: as the host of whatever this thing was, I was instructed to award a cash prize of $250,000 to the "winning" boat, on camera. The ingenious producer who came up with the idea was not in Dutch Harbor when the commander of the Coast Guard found out about it, but I was.

"Are you people out of your minds?"

It was a general question, posed to a small group of producers, cameramen, and me.

"Gentlemen, this is the most dangerous job on the planet. How much deadlier do you want it to be?"

The commander was looking directly at me. In the ensuing silence, it seemed rude not to reply.

"Well, sir, I can't speak for the network, but it seems to me—"

"What's your name, son?"

The commander was my age but called me "son." How awesome is that?

"I'm Mike Rowe," I said.

"Are you the star of the show?"

"No, I'm the host."

"Do you work for the Discovery Channel?"

"Yes, sir, I do."

"Then why the hell can't you speak for them?"

I understood the commander's frustration. Every week, the Coast Guard answers multiple calls from fishing boats in distress, boats captained by mortal men who sometimes push things a little too far in the race to get as much crab on board as quickly as possible. In the commander's eyes, we were morons who'd flown in from Hollywood to throw gas on a fire that was already burning out of control.

The commander wasn't entirely wrong.

"Trust me," I said. "I'm sure that my masters won't want to turn your crab season into a free-for-all."

The commander sighed and shook his head. "You don't get it, son. It's already a free-for-all. And you guys are making it worse."

Once again, he wasn't wrong to worry: the act of watching a thing always changes the behavior of the thing you're watching. It's called the "observer effect." It's true in physics, and it's true in crab fishing. With or without $250,000 to dish out, a film crew in Dutch was going to change things. But the commander wasn't entirely right, either.

Two weeks after this conversation, the *Big Valley* went down. But there was no film crew on board. No one was there to watch as it sank. And, injuries and fatalities *didn't* increase after filming began. In fact, after our first season aired, a new law was passed that eliminated the derby approach that many believed made crab fishing more dangerous than it had to be. I *could* argue that our show actually helped make things safer. But I won't, because people still die up there, no matter how careful they try to be.

You can't script the Bering Sea.

As for duck farts, those are easy: Kahlúa, Bailey's, and whiskey. Layered in equal parts just in that order. They were Phil's favorite, but, as I told him so many times, there's no accounting for taste.

A LITTLE TOWN UP NORTH

During her farewell tour in 2005, Cher demanded that multiple boxes of aloe vera tissues in rose-scented, cube-shaped boxes be placed in her dressing room at every stop.

Happily, Cher wasn't David's problem.

When Mariah Carey was interviewed on British TV in 2009, she demanded to be lowered onto the sofa by two stagehands—so that she wouldn't crease her dress.

Happily, Mariah wasn't David's problem.

When Madonna checked into a 5,000-square-foot hotel suite in 2012, she demanded hundreds of pink roses, individually placed into hundreds of crystal vases, carefully situated on every flat surface.

Happily, Madonna wasn't David's problem, either.

But when Eddie demanded seven full weeks to prepare, well . . . that *was* David's problem. Because if David was going to pull off an event of this magnitude—the most ambitious outdoor gathering in recent memory—he'd need the right entertainment. And there was really no one else like Eddie. But seven *weeks* of rehearsal? That was a diva move unlike anything David had ever experienced. The event

was less than a month away. Moving the date at this point would be a logistical nightmare. What to do?

David rubbed his aching temples and took a moment to feel sorry for himself. Back in the sixties, prima donnas were no less common than they are today—and guys like David were still at their mercy. But the sixties were also the reason David was determined to make this happen. America was at war, young people were feeling rebellious, and David thought the country could benefit from a massive expression of love and unity. He also believed the farmland around his hometown would be the perfect venue.

Of course, he was right.

You know the town. You might even know the famous address. But unless you were there in person to hear the music and smell the air and lose yourself in the moment, it's easy to forget that the whole event turned on a single performance—which is why David ultimately agreed to Eddie's demand. He rebooked the vendors, rebooked the performers, redrew the permits, and announced a new date. Then he prayed that Eddie would come through. Which, of course, Eddie did.

Again, you had to be there. But if you weren't, it's fair to say that Eddie was a force of nature. Like Hendrix and Joplin, he could go for hours on end. Like the Grateful Dead and Jefferson Airplane, he could riff in ways that left audiences astounded and begging for more. But unlike those famous headliners, Eddie didn't have a band to back him up. When Eddie took the stage, it was just him. That's why no one wanted to follow Eddie—not ever. That's also why, in spite of the last-minute scheduling change, the announcement of his involvement triggered a migration of people. Thousands walked, thousands hitchhiked, and thousands more did whatever was necessary to get themselves to that little town up north, where they hoped to be a part of something bigger than themselves and maybe hear something transcendent. Something they'd always remember. And boy, did they ever.

After a few very solid opening acts, Eddie took the stage—and the crowd went wild. For two hours, the most electrifying performer in America held thousands of people in the palm of his hand. They cheered and they wept, and when Eddie had finished, they applauded for a full fifteen minutes, deeply moved and profoundly grateful to know that one day they would tell their grandchildren, "I was there the day that Eddie made history."

Of course, they did. To this day, their descendants are passing the same story on to their children. Because, remember, this was the sixties. A time when America was at war, and young people were feeling rebellious. A time when a farmer named David had the good sense to see that the farmland around his hometown would be a perfect venue for his carefully planned expression of love and unity. Of course, he was right. A few months earlier, another kind of gathering had unfolded in that very same place: a gathering that brought 175,000 young people together for three days of unforgettable slaughter. An epic bloodbath that left 50,000 Americans dead or wounded. Many of them were still scattered, in terrible pieces, right there on David's front lawn.

That's why, after three months of unspeakable cleanup, David was determined to dedicate the farmland around his home to those now buried beneath it. And so he did. But unless you were actually there to hear the bands play their dirges, to hear the choirs sing their hymns—unless you were there to smell the air, still rank with rotting flesh, and listen to Eddie deliver his 13,000-word eulogy from memory, it's hard to imagine what happened in that little town up north, during that unforgettable summer of death.

You know the town. And you probably know the address. No—not the two-hour rhetorical masterpiece no one thought they'd ever forget—but the two-minute rumination that followed: a shockingly brief, 272-word homily that left most people scratching their heads, wondering if they had missed something.

Funny how things work out. Edward Everett was once known as America's Greatest Orator. But today very few people remember him at all. Fewer still can recall a single phrase from the epic address he delivered so masterfully on that sacred afternoon, in 1863. No one at all still recalls David Wills, the man who organized the event that transformed the farmland around his home into the sprawling National Cemetery it is today. But we all remember the man who stole the show seven score and sixteen years ago. A haggard man, suffering from fever and grieving the death of his son. A humble man, about as far from a diva as a politician could be. An honest man, who was content to write *his* speech on the morning of the event in the spare bedroom of David Wills's home.

A man named Lincoln, who delivered the address we do remember: a famous address that took its name from a little town up north. A little town called . . . Gettysburg.

TLDR

Those were the letters that appeared in the comments under my very first Facebook post, back in whatever year that was. I didn't know what they meant, but they kept showing up after all of my subsequent posts: TLDR.

TL/DR

tl:dr

TL>;<DR

I encountered a millennial one day, out on the mean streets of San Francisco, and asked him what these letters meant.

"Too long, didn't read."

"You're kidding," I said. "Why would someone with no time take time to tell me that they had no time?"

The millennial shrugged and said, "People are busy?"

"I understand that," I said. "But if you have time to spell out the fact that you're too busy to read what I wrote, how busy can you really be?"

But the millennial was no longer listening. He had leaned down to pet Freddy, who snarled viciously and tried to bite his finger off. *That* got the millennial's attention.

"Hey, man! You should tell people your dog is mean!"

"I'm sorry," I said. "I didn't have time."

I wonder sometimes if Freddy is smarter than he lets on. Like Lincoln at Gettysburg, he made his point in no time. With a snarl and a snap, he gave his audience something to remember. My dog seems to understand the power of brevity. But do I? Have I held your attention thus far? Or have I droned on like Edward Everett, bela-boring things unnecessarily?

Don't get me wrong: what Everett did at Gettysburg was remark-able. He wrote 13,000 words, memorized them, and then delivered them flawlessly to a full house. His performance was hailed as a tri-umph in both the Union and the Confederacy. This was a man who could have talked about a pencil for eight minutes, or eighty, and for that he has my deepest admiration. But I wonder how Everett would do in our TL/DR culture. I wonder, how would he do at a TED conference?

You might be familiar with TED: a series of gatherings in Sili-con Valley where self-styled "creatives" pay thousands of dollars to hear luminaries hold forth on topics near and dear to their hearts. Many famous people have given TED Talks, though the most popu-lar ones tend to come from people you've probably never heard of. They have titles like "How to Measure Your Life"; "My Stroke of Insight"; "The Skill of Self-Confidence." Makes you wonder how creative those creatives are.

I gave a TED Talk, too, in 2008. Like Lincoln, who was invited to Gettysburg to make some "remarks," I didn't know I'd been invited to give an actual speech. I thought I was there to say a few words on behalf of the Discovery Channel, which was sponsoring the event. In reality, Discovery had volunteered me to give a presentation about the dignity of dirty jobs. An eighteen-minute presentation—no more, no less.

I called my speech "The Changing Face of the Modern-Day Proletariat" and used my eighteen minutes onstage to reflect on castration—specifically, the oral castration of baby lambs. It was a popular talk. You can watch it on YouTube right now. As a matter of fact, you should. Go ahead, I'll wait.

Are you back? Great. As you just saw, the process of biting the testicles off a baby lamb is not as barbaric as you might have thought. Sure, it's disgusting, but it's a lot more pleasant than the method recommended by experts at the Humane Society, who assured me that putting a tight rubber band around the scrotum is the way to go. That process takes days and causes prolonged agony for the lamb but *looks* a lot more civilized than the toothier method. It's "approved." But it's not more effective. Nor is it better, in any way, for the lamb.

Anyway, I told my story with way more detail than my audience might have expected. Naturally, I cast myself as the protagonist. Then I discussed Aristotle's ideas about "anagnorisis," wherein the hero discovers something about himself—an inescapable truth that he didn't know—and "peripeteia," whereby that discovery reverses the course of the narrative.

When Oedipus, for instance, learns that he enjoys having sex with older women, that's anagnorisis: a discovery about himself. When he discovers that the woman sharing his bed is his mother, that's peripeteia. Likewise, when Bruce Willis, in *The Sixth Sense*, realizes that little Cole really can see dead people, that's anagnorisis. When Bruce realizes Cole can see *him*—because he's been dead all along—that's peripeteia.

I liked the idea of using Aristotle's high-minded terms to describe the surprising truth about biting the balls off baby lambs. Specifically: I liked using those terms to illustrate my realization that, sometimes, the experts don't know their ass from a hot rock. But let me tell you: I would have liked it a lot more if I had been given two hours instead of eighteen minutes to explain myself.

Here's something you might not know about TED Talks: many of them exceed the allotted time. Take it from a guy who sat through three days of these things: otherwise brilliant people struggle mightily to keep their stories under eighteen minutes. Those are the TED Talks that never get posted to YouTube. The ones that make me feel better about how much trouble I had with mine. In fact, you may have noticed: despite my best efforts, I also went over the allotted length—by two whole minutes. No big deal, right? Except that two minutes was all Lincoln needed to unite a divided country—to make the occasion eternal with words we now consider immortal.

Words that, if posted on Facebook today, would undoubtedly elicit a "TL/DR" from those with just seconds to spare.

Or maybe a "Woof!" from Freddy.

SOMETHING
UNFORGETTABLE AND REAL

A high-performance convertible flies down a two-lane highway at speeds well in excess of the posted limits. In hot pursuit, a professional stuntman drives a Ford station wagon that's pulling an empty trailer. The scene couldn't be simpler: No special effects, no CGI, just a good, old-fashioned Hollywood car chase.

On his deathbed, thirty-one years later, Bill Hickman recalls the scene in vivid detail. In his mind's eye, he can still see the convertible rounding the corner and disappearing from view. He can still feel the frustration at not being able to catch up. If he had been driving his famous Dodge Charger that day—the muscle car he drove in *Bullitt*—things might have ended differently.

Bill smiles at the memory. The Charger had been one hell of a car and *Bullitt* one hell of a movie. As the film's stunt coordinator, Bill had been asked to create the most realistic car chase ever filmed. By most accounts he'd done just that. With Steve McQueen in hot pursuit, driving a Ford Mustang 390, the two men turned the hills of San Francisco into their personal racetrack, complete with hairpin turns and asphalt launching pads. Their muscle cars literally flew through the air. Hubcaps exploded from their wheels and rolled crazily down the streets, and the fiery explosion at the end—when Bill's car crashes into the gas pumps at the filling station—set a new standard on the big screen for vehicular verisimilitude.

It was the mistakes, though—along with the actual stunts—that brought a new sense of realism to every Bill Hickman sequence. In one shot, Bill sideswipes a parked car with a camera affixed to it, knocking it sideways. Normally, footage like that would wind up on the cutting room floor, but Bill argued that the mistake made the

chase feel more real, and the director agreed. The shot stayed in, and *Bullitt* won an Oscar.

After that, every director in Hollywood wanted a car chase with the "Hickman touch." In *The Seven-Ups*, Bill drove his Pontiac Grand Ville

so aggressively that the actor in the passenger seat screamed in terror. That was not in the script. But the director kept it in—because it was real.

During *The French Connection*, the door of a parked car opens seconds before Bill speeds by at sixty miles per hour, ripping the door off its hinges. This, too, looks shockingly real—because it *is* real. So, too, was a severed door that went spiraling through the air like a giant ninja star, nearly decapitating the camera crew and sending passersby diving for cover.

In that same sequence, Hickman—doubling Gene Hackman—chases down a bad guy who's commandeered an El train in Brooklyn. The stunt takes place fifty feet below the speeding train, as Hickman's 1971 Pontiac LeMans tries to keep pace on a busy New York street. It was a difficult scene to shoot, and the director hated the first take. He told Hickman that he wanted a car chase that would scare the hell out of audiences: something unforgettable and real.

Bill smiles, ruefully, at the memory, recalling his exact conversation with the famous director.

"You want real?" he said. "Meet me tomorrow morning at the corner of Eighty-sixth and Stillwell. Bring your camera, if you have the balls for it. I'll show you something real." The next morning, William Friedkin strapped himself and his camera into the back seat of Hickman's LeMans and captured some of the most harrowing footage ever to make it onto the big screen. Why? Because Hickman exceeded speeds of 90 mph—in actual New York City traffic. No special effects. No CGI. And no permit. The result? *Six* Oscars for *The French Connection* and a sequence Friedkin—the man who directed *The Exorcist*—would call "the scariest thing I've ever seen."

Now, as he lies dying, Bill comes to realize an inescapable truth about his own identity: his whole life has been one long car chase. In his final moments, he thinks about how far Hollywood has come from the days in which actors sat behind fake windshields and fake steering wheels and pretended to drive as fake footage rolled by. He also thinks about how lucky he's been over the years. It's a miracle that no one has ever been hurt during any of his scenes—unless, of course, you count that very first scene, thirty-one years ago, back when Bill was a young stuntman driving a station wagon, hauling an empty trailer, trying to keep up with that speeding convertible.

Bill can still see the convertible rounding the corner and disappearing from view. He can still feel his frustration at not being able to catch up. And he can still see the sight that awaits him when he finally does round that corner: slumped behind the wheel of the mangled sports car, he sees the young driver who should have been sitting beside him. A driver whose Porsche should have been secured on the empty trailer behind his station wagon as they drove to the

Salinas Speedway. Alas, the kid had insisted upon driving himself to warm up the car's engine for the race he was scheduled to run that afternoon.

It was a scene, all right—but this was no movie, and with no director on hand to say "cut," the action had unfolded in slow motion, as real life sometimes does. Bill had run to the wreck and pulled his young protégé from the smoldering pile of twisted steel. There were no last words. No final close-ups. Just the sound of one ultimate exhalation, seconds before the driver died in Bill's arms and everything faded to black.

That was the start of a legendary career—the career of a stuntman remembered for his obsession with making action movies feel unforgettable and real—along with the start of a legend. The legend of a twenty-four-year-old race car driver whose fleeting work on the big screen is still remembered as something real and unforgettable. A rebel without a cause named . . . James Dean.

How crazy is this: just a few weeks before the accident, James Dean recorded a public service announcement advising young drivers to slow down. He stared into the camera and said, "The life you save just might be mine." Then, just two *hours* before the crash that killed him, a cop pulled him over and gave him a speeding ticket. Do you think the universe was trying to tell him something?

I don't know. I doubt that Bill Hickman knew. But what I *can* tell you is this: Back in 2002, I wasn't searching for signs from the universe. I was too busy impersonating a host every night on *Evening Magazine.*

"Good evening, folks! I'm Mike Rowe, and tonight we're at the Mondavi Vineyard in beautiful Napa Valley, home to the finest wines in all the world!"

"Good evening, folks! I'm Mike Rowe, and tonight we're at the

Snodgrass Apple Orchard in scenic Pescadero, home to the finest apples in all the world!"

"Good evening, folks! I'm Mike Rowe, and tonight we're at Eddie's Electronic Emporium in beautiful downtown Burlingame, where you can save a bundle on your next big-screen TV!"

Never mind Steve McQueen flying through the mean streets of San Francisco in his souped-up Mustang. Imagine, instead, a forty-two-year-old B-list celebrity, racing along the same streets in a Lincoln Navigator (*The Official SUV of Evening Magazine!*) stuffed with swag: free wine, free apples, free TVs—free whatever I could get my hands on.

"Good evening, folks! I'm Mike Rowe, and tonight we're coming to you from Futon World in picturesque Alameda, home of the Bay Area's very best futons!"

Do you have any idea how hard it is to strap a free futon onto the roof of your free Navigator?

Fact is, for a guy who had lost all his money, starring in a show like *Evening* was just what the doctor ordered. I got free tickets to every show in town, free nights in fancy hotels, free meals in five-star restaurants, and free clothes from Macy's (*The Official Provider of Mike Rowe's Wardrobe!*). It was like QVC, only this time I got to keep all the stuff I was hawking—including my aforementioned gigantic head, cast in bronze. Not what you'd call a fulfilling time, but I wasn't searching for meaning. I was just trying to get back on my feet, and all that free crap made me feel a lot better—until, one day, the universe *did* call. Luckily, I picked up the phone.

"Oh. Hi, Mom. How's it going?"

"Well, your father's up on the roof doing God knows what, and I'm afraid he's going to fall off. But I'm fine."

Never once has my mother answered this simple question without first telling me what my father was doing. Then she got to the point.

"I'm calling about your grandfather. He's ninety years old, you know, and won't be around forever. I was thinking how nice it would be if, just once, he could turn on his television and see you doing something that looks like work."

Mothers. They can be so cruel.

"Well, thanks, Mom. What did you have in mind?"

"Oh, I don't know," she said. "How about a logging camp? Or a dairy farm? Or, maybe, a coal mine?"

"It's California, Mom. Coal's illegal out here."

"Well, I'm sure you'll come up with something," she said. "Where are you shooting this evening?"

"I believe tonight's episode will be coming to you from a Tea Room in Chinatown."

"Oh my," she said. "Doesn't that sound exciting. Your grandfather will be riveted."

That night, I drove back from Chinatown with my Navigator bursting with complimentary tins of Jasmine Dragon Pearls (*The Official Tea of Evening Magazine!*). Along the way, I thought about our conversation. It had been a while since I'd talked to my pop, and I missed him. Surely, there was room in our show for a segment that he could relate to. Why *not* mix things up a bit?

And so, the next morning, after a free haircut at Diepetro/Todd (*The Official Hair Stylists of Evening Magazine!*), I drove all around San Francisco, trying to see the town through my grandfather's eyes. There were no logging camps or dairy farms or mines of any kind. Just boutiques and cafés and artisanal what-nots. But the answer to my mother's question was there, all the same—right under my feet. I didn't know it, but it had been there all along. . . .

THE STAR OF THE SHOW

Our hero was knee-deep in a rancid river, far below the city he called home. Accompanying him was his loyal cameraman, Branson, along with his guide—a sewer inspector whose name he didn't know. The men were dressed in orange overalls, rubber hip boots, and yellow hardhats. The inspector carried a bucket that hung from a rope looped around his neck. Our hero followed, and Branson brought up the rear, weighed down by his camera and a microphone attached to a long pole.

"Be careful," the inspector said. "It's slicker than snot through here. If you slip, it's better to fall backwards."

This was excellent advice. The flux that flowed through these ancient tunnels was filled with the flotsam and jetsam of a million medicine cabinets: tampons and Q-tips, diapers and dental floss, Kotex and Kleenex and condoms that clung to the men's rubber boots like colored ornaments on an X-rated Christmas tree.

"How much further?" our hero gasped.

"Not far," said the inspector. "Another hundred yards."

The trio went deeper into the labyrinth. The tunnel narrowed, and the lights on their helmets revealed red brick walls that seemed to undulate in the gloom. Was our hero hallucinating? Was it a trick of the light, or a phantasm brought on by the stench? No. It was roaches. Millions of roaches, feasting on a permanent glaze of human excrement. Drawn by their headlamps, like moths to a flame, they rushed over to greet the men, covering our hero in a blanket of rippling vermin. He was disgusted, but determined to do his job. And so, turning to Branson's camera, he addressed his viewers:

"Good evening, folks . . ."

But that's as far as he got before a thumb-sized roach crawled into his mouth, causing him to gag and sputter.

"Try not to talk," the inspector said. "Nothing good happens down here when your mouth is open."

This, too, was excellent advice, but our hero could not heed it, for talking was his job and the sound of his own voice enchanted him. Turning once more to Branson's camera, he started again:

"Funny thing about sewers," he said, but never got to the punchline. A blast of coffee-colored wastewater had erupted from a small hole in the wall, shellacking the bonnier side of his chiseled visage.

"See what I mean?" said the inspector.

Strange popping sounds filled the air as toilets in Nob Hill, above them, were flushed. Left and right, liquids exploded from hidden pipes that were called "laterals." Our hero knew all about laterals. Before entering the sewer, he'd filled his head with all sorts of effluvia to share with his audience. That, too, was part of his job: to know all there was to know about various subjects, and share his expertise.

But the sewer was not cooperating.

The men pressed on, duck-walking through this shooting gallery of human scat. Pressing through the muck. Pushing through the mire. Splashing their way through a three-dimensional fresco of macrobiotic devastation that only Dante could have divined. Finally, they rounded a corner and arrived at a crossroads where two tunnels converged.

"This whole area needs work," the inspector said, as he wiped an army of roaches away from the ceiling. "See these rotten bricks in the arch? They all have to come out."

But our hero was not listening. He was looking again into the lens of Branson's camera, and clearing his throat.

"The walls around me were built in 1866," he explained in a crisp, well-modulated baritone. "And today, you'll find over a thousand miles of tunnels down here, all of which—"

Just then, a sewer rat emerged from the miasma and crept up behind him, as rats often do. He was the size of a shoebox—plump and wet and reeking of urine. In a twinkling, the rodent scampered onto our hero's back and up to his shoulder. There he paused, perched like a parrot, squealed into our hero's ear, and dove into his lap. Squealing back, our hero leapt to his feet, smashed his head into the low ceiling, then fell face-first into the sludge as a curtain of roaches rained down upon him.

Never mind Dante. This was a page only Poe could have penned. A portrait that only Bosch could have painted. This was a baptism in a river of shit.

Our hero pushed himself up from the sludge and tried to recall the difference between hepatitis A and B. Not that it mattered—surely he had contracted both. For once, he was speechless. But the sewer inspector was not.

"Hey, Chief. When you're done screwing around with the local wildlife, I could use some help over here. Grab that trowel, would ya, and mix me a new batch of grout?"

Our hero sighed. Why not? The sewer had thwarted him at every turn. If he could not do his job, perhaps he could do someone else's?

"Thanks," the inspector said, taking the trowel.

For the first time, our hero looked—really looked—at the inspector. The man was in his late thirties with blond hair. He was breathing hard, drenched in sweat, but good-humored. His name was Gene. It said so, right there on his work shirt.

"Please tell me they pay you a fortune."

The inspector laughed and hammered his chisel deep into the rotten grout.

"I wouldn't call it a fortune," he said, "but I'm doing pretty well."

"How about the smell? Do you ever get used to it?"

"A man can get used to anything," Gene said.

For the next hour, our hero forgot all about the camera and worked as the inspector's apprentice. He hammered out bricks. He mixed grout. He bumbled and fumbled and got more wrong than right, but he tried, and that's when it happened. There, at the subterranean crossroads, covered in poop and taking orders, our hero finally realized he wasn't the star of the show. The real star was Gene—the modest sewer inspector working beside him.

Thus began a new chapter in the life of our humbled hero, who was inspired in that moment to create a new kind of show. A show with a mission instead of a script; a guest instead of a host. A show you may have seen, that led to a podcast you may have listened to, and a book that you'll probably finish today. Unless, of course, you decide to go back to the beginning—which would please our hero to no end . . .

Anyway, that's the way I heard it.

See what I did there? I turned myself into a hero. You should try it sometime. All you have to do is put yourself on a pedestal and write about yourself in the third person. Be careful, though—when you cast yourself as the star of your own show, it's easy to see everyone else as a bit player in the story of your life. That's what happened to me. After I lost my safety net, I became disconnected from all sorts of things, including the people around me. Until my unplanned baptism in the sewers of San Francisco, I didn't even know Gene's name. But, thanks to him (and to Branson, who never stopped rolling), I left that day with footage that inspired the first episode of *Dirty Jobs*, a show that allowed me to tell the stories of people like my grandfather, not through the eyes of a host who pretends to know more than he does, but through the eyes of the new guy, whose first day on the job is every day.

That would have made my pop proud.

Speaking of heroes, at the start of this book I promised to revisit Paul Harvey—and as I might have mentioned, a promise made is a debt unpaid. So let's get to it: Paul Harvey was a hero to me. The son of a cop who'd been killed by two robbers, he worked his way up from being an office boy at a radio station in Tulsa, Oklahoma, to hosting the popular radio show that inspired my podcast. For thirty-three years, he told us *The Rest of the Story*, and the way I remember it, he *always* put his subjects first.

Obviously, I can't fill Paul Harvey's shoes. But I can follow in his footsteps, and I've tried to do so in these pages, writing about the people who interest me most. Sadly, many of those people are dead, including a few I knew personally. Joan Rivers, Dick Clark, and Tony Bourdain can no longer tell their own stories. Like Fred King, they live now only in my memory, and the memories of the many people they touched. I'm grateful to have known them all.

Kippy Stroud, too, has shuffled off her mortal coil. I didn't know her well, but I was happy to spend a year in her haunted mansion. I hope that she and her dad have finally reconciled and forgiven me for permanently borrowing all twenty-one Travis McGee mysteries, which I've since read and re-read no less than twenty-one times.

Happily, my dog, Freddy, is alive and well as of this writing, and mostly continent. So too are my dear parents, John and Peggy. Dad's still volunteering at the hospital, delivering Meals on Wheels, and strutting around on the stage. Mom's still searching for typos on my Facebook page and working on her second book. May they continue to do so for another hundred years.

Sandy is still pissed off at the Russians for sending Laika into space, but pleased to see me publish an actual book. "Nice to see you finally write something you get paid for," she says. "Think anybody'll read it?"

That's a very good question.

Chuck Klausmeyer, my buddy from high school, still wears that terrible blue blazer he loaned me twenty years ago—even though it no longer fits. He also produces my podcast, in spite of my repeated warnings about working for old friends. Likewise, the Irish Hammer is still on the case, doing her best to keep me from becoming an asshole—or, worse, *looking* like one. This last chapter, for instance, has led to some gentle interrogation.

"Tell me," she says, "will you be referring to yourself in the third person from now on? Will you require a new pedestal? And what should I call you? Do you prefer 'My Hero' or 'Your Majesty'?"

I've assured her that either is fine.

Grumpy's is still there, but Johnny's is no more, and Baltimore's a worse place for its absence. Sadly, the Baltimore Opera Company is also kaput. Michael Gellert, my buddy who greased the wheels at my first audition, now directs the Harbor City Music Company, one of the very best a cappella women's choruses in the world. The Chorus of the Chesapeake lives on as well, directed now by Fred King's son, Kevin. The old guard is mostly gone, but a new batch of men are singing the same songs in four-part harmony, at a volume consistent with that of a Metallica concert.

Shortly after I left CBS to work on *Dirty Jobs*, *Evening Magazine* went off the air. I'm told my departure and the show's demise were purely coincidental. QVC, on the other hand, is alive and well, reaching into over 100 million homes and generating billions of dollars in annual sales. I haven't always spoken about my tenure there with reverence, but the truth is, everything I needed to know about this business I learned there. For that, I'm indebted. I suppose I should also thank the rat. We're no longer in touch, but thanks to his timely intervention, I wound up with more than a hit show. I wound up with a foundation and something that looks very much like a career.

Speaking of rats, the trusted financial adviser who stole my money finally went to jail, and deservedly so. But I can't tell you I was a completely innocent victim. Deep down, I suspected the figures he presented might be too good to be true, but I kept my head in the sand and told myself the story I wanted to believe. Lesson learned.

I also promised, at the outset, to tell you the truth, the way I heard it. And for the most part, I think I have. But of course, the truth and the whole truth are never the same—and that brings me back to Phil Harris. He suffered a massive stroke, in 2010, and ended up in a hospital bed, dying, unable to speak. Todd Stanley, the cameraman who had filmed him for years, was there with him. Todd's camera was off, out of respect. But Phil motioned Todd to his bedside and scribbled a few words on a scrap of paper: "You've got to get the end of the story."

And so, Todd Stanley picked up his camera and the millions of people who'd gotten to share Phil's life came together to share in his death. Kind of extraordinary, right? Even . . . heroic?

Phil Harris believed a story without an ending wasn't really a story.

Paul Harvey believed a story wasn't over until you heard the rest of it.

The way I see it, both were correct.

Regarding Paul Harvey and the rest of *his* story: He passed away, too, a year before Phil Harris did. He was one of the few broadcasters ever to receive the Presidential Medal of Freedom. Not long ago, I heard from his son. Paul Harvey Jr. wrote and produced *The Rest of the Story* for his dad, and when his letter arrived at my office, I was afraid to open it. For all I knew, it was a cease-and-desist order regarding my podcast.

But it wasn't. It was a very kind note, along with a generous check for the mikeroweWORKS foundation. According to Paul Jr., his dad would have liked the work we were doing. Modesty aside, that was a proud and humbling moment for me—one more thing to be grateful for.

Finally, a point of clarity regarding Jon Stewart. I dropped his name earlier because I wanted to circle back later and tell you about the time I was hired to host *The Daily Show*—not once, but twice. It's an interesting story, but my friend Alex (a wreck of a man and one heck of a writer) says that my book is already too long. His instincts have proven useful—so far, anyway—so I guess I'll save that one for another day. Instead, I'll just say, for the record, that I did meet Jon Stewart, once upon a time, way back in 2006. I was a guest on *The Daily Show*, answering Jon's trenchant and insightful questions. Questions like "So tell us, Mike, what was your dirtiest job?"

The way I heard it, Jon Stewart called my answer "the funniest thing he'd ever heard." But you can watch our interview on YouTube and judge for yourself.

In fact, I think you should.

Go ahead. Google it.

I'll wait . . .

ACKNOWLEDGMENTS

When Jennifer Bergstrom over at Simon & Schuster first encouraged me to write a book, I told her I'd get back to her. Ten years later, I did, and learned to my surprise that her offer was still good. I'm grateful to Jen for her extraordinary patience with me, along with the support of her excellent team—Karyn Marcus, Aimee Bell, Jennifer Long, Molly Gregory, Jennifer Robinson, John Vairo, Caroline Pallotta, Steve Breslin, and Jaime Putorti—all of whom tolerated my endless rewrites and chronic disregard for internal deadlines with understanding and good humor.

I'm equally indebted to everyone at mikeroweWORKS—in particular, Mary Sullivan, Chuck Klausmeyer, and Jade Estrada, who looked on in horror as I vanished from view for several months to impersonate a writer and wondered, quite rightly, if I would ever return. Without their loyalty and support, this book would not exist. I'm also grateful to Sean McCourt and Susan Lee Smith, whose early ideas for my podcast have found their way into the preceding pages. I'm much obliged to you both.

Alex Abramovich (a wreck of a man and one heck of a writer)

was instrumental in assembling and shaping the preceding pages. Alex also recommended I use Marcellus Hall to provide the illustrations, which I think are terrific. Thank you both for making this book better than it would have otherwise been.

Finally, I'd like to thank the listeners of *The Way I Heard It,* and the five million people who continue to frequent my Facebook page. Of my many masters, you are the ones that matter most, with the notable exception of my parents, to whom this book is dedicated, and without whom I'd have no one to acknowledge.

ABOUT THE AUTHOR

Mike Rowe is best known as the executive producer and host of the hit shows *Dirty Jobs*, *Somebody's Gotta Do It*, and *Returning the Favor*. He also hosts the podcast *The Way I Heard It*, a collection of stories for the "curious mind with a short attention span." As CEO of the mikeroweWORKS foundation, Mike has led the effort to close America's widening skills gap and facilitated the granting of millions of dollars for work-ethic scholarships.